A HISTORY
TEACHING
TOOLBOX

Practical strategies for the secondary classroom

Russel Tarr

RUSSEL TARR

First published 2016

Typeset in Garamond

All photographs by the author

Copyright © 2016 Russel Tarr

ISBN: 1508512051
ISBN-13: 978-1508512059

For Marie-Anne

RUSSEL TARR

CONTENTS

HOW TO USE THIS BOOK

This book provides history teachers in secondary schools with simple, practical and creative strategies to improve engagement and subject mastery in the classroom. It is broken into key sections to broadly reflect various stages in the learning process. Although the case studies I outline will refer to examples from the history classroom, many of the strategies behind them will, I hope, be easily transferable to other subjects.

As a simple target, I suggest you aim to use one key idea from each of the chapters within the academic year, preferably with different year groups. The following year, decide which ones to keep, which to refine, and which to ditch – as well as which fresh ideas you would like to try out.

All of the templates I refer to within the book can be downloaded via my blog "Tarr's Toolbox" (www.tarrstoolbox.net) where I share teaching strategies that have worked particularly well in my own classroom. The book also draws heavily on resources I have shared on my training courses and developed on my websites www.activehistory.co.uk and www.classtools.net, through which you can contact me directly for further support.

Russel Tarr
@russeltarr / @activehistory / @classtools

RUSSEL TARR

1

IMPARTING KNOWLEDGE TO STUDENTS

Rigorously imparting subject knowledge to students is a fundamental priority. This chapter outlines means of doing so which keep students actively engaged rather than relying solely on 'chalk and talk' teacher lectures.

Chronological narratives

At the start of a new topic, it's often useful to provide students with an essential chronology of events before analysing this timeline in terms of key questions. Simply delivering a narrative lecture to the class gives the students too much opportunity to lose attention. The following strategies help students engage with and absorb the narrative, and can be used in sequence or in isolation.

1. Running dictation

The running dictation is an efficient and energetic way of teaching students about dramatic moments in history.

- Before the lesson, anticipate dividing the class into teams of about five students and print off a timeline of key events for each team. This timeline should be written in the present tense (e.g. "The Spanish Armada has just set sail for England!") to give it a sense of immediacy.
- Cut the first timeline into slips and place these neatly into an envelope with the first event at the top of the pile. Repeat for the other timelines.
- When the class arrives, divide the students into their groups. Each group member should be given a number (1, 2, 3…)
- When the activity begins, position yourself at the far end of the classroom (even better, go outside where there is more space).
- Upon your signal, the first person from each team should run up to you and collect their first slip from their timeline.
- They should run back to their teams and read the slip out to their group. The rest of the team writes quick notes. The speaker can repeat details, but cannot show the slip to the team.
- When you get the impression that the teams have had almost enough time, announce that the next slip of information is available. The second person from each team should run to you, bringing the original slip with them. They exchange this for the

next slip from the timeline, and return to their teams.

- The process is then repeated until all the slips have been used up, with responsibility for 'running' looping through the students in each group for as long as necessary.
- When the process is completed, students should return to the classroom and spend some time in their groups comparing and completing their notes: after all, each member of the team will not have notes relating to events that they read to the rest of the group.

2. What do you think they should do next?

The running dictation is less effective for detailed, slow-paced stories which take place over many years. A better method in this case is a teacher-led lecture using the 'What should they do next?' format. This is particularly good for topics based around the assessment of a particular individual's handling of a situation. For example, when studying how far the Russian Provisional Government was responsible for its own downfall in October 1917, I introduce a dilemma that they face upon taking power on a PowerPoint slide. I then discuss with the class what the appropriate response should be to increase support for the government (sometimes providing them with several options):

1. February

- The Tsar has been arrested and placed under house arrest, but **The PG lacks real power**. The Petrograd Soviet has issued "Order Number 1" which asserts control over the armed forces. The Minister of War has stated that "The PG has no real power...it exists only as long as it is permitted to do so by the Soviet".

- *To the PG:*
- *You must decide who should be your Prime Minister. Do you select*
- *(a) Kerensky (a member of both the Soviet and the Duma) or*
- *(b) Prince Lvov, a moderate aristocrat?*
- *Why?*

Remember: your objective is to decide which choice would increase your level of popular support!

I then move to the next slide which reveals what the government actually did. Based on the earlier discussion, students then make brief notes on how successfully they think the situation was handled, using a grid which is already getting them to think in terms of themes rather than a chronological narrative:

As the teacher leads this exercise, organise notes under these four headings.
Note: To save time, you should just note the NUMBER of each event first (with explanation of why placed in that cell if necessary). At the end of the exercise you can then be given the PowerPoint presentation to develop your notes in more detail.

	Bolsheviks = "Methods"		Provisional Government = "Conditions"	
	Lenin		Kerensky	
	a. Evidence of Popularity [Fitzpatrick]	b. Evidence of Unpopularity [Pipes]	c. Evidence of Popularity [Pipes]	d. Evidence of Unpopularity [Fitzpatrick]
Military: The Soldiers				
Socio-Economic: The Soviets, Peasants				
Political: Other parties (Mensheviks, SRs etc)				

The process is repeated for other events – sometimes calling upon students to consider how the Provisional Government should act, and sometimes considering how the Bolsheviks should react.

After the teacher-led element is finished, students can be provided with the complete PowerPoint presentation to develop their tables further: if students are aware that you are going to do this from the outset, this is an efficient strategy to ensure that during the lesson they are focusing on formulating and writing judgments, rather than furiously trying to copy the factual information in each slide word for word.

3. Re-assemble a timeline in the correct order

This strategy is most effective for simpler timelines with relatively few events. I use it frequently with younger classes in a quiz format to get them engaged. Start by providing students with a list of events running down the page. To the right of the events are columns like this:

	Event	My Guess	Correct Answer	Difference
William has himself crowned as King of England				
Godwineson swears to support William's claim				
Edward the Confessor dies childless				

In "my guess" students number each event to reflect the chronological order in which they think they occurred (with "1" being the first event, and so on). Afterwards, the teacher then tells the class what the "correct answer" is for each event. Students then calculate the difference between the two numbers (note: this will always be a positive number – e.g. 5-3 would be a difference of 2, and 3-5 would also be a difference of 2). They then add up the total of the "difference" column to get an overall score: the student with the lowest overall difference is the winner!

One important point with this technique is that some thought should be given to providing some contextual clues within each "event" about what happened previously, or what is about to happen next (e.g. "Because Harold promised to support William, he was then allowed to go home to England").

4. Categorise, colour-code, elaborate and chunk

Following on from the above (or, with timelines that are too complex or detailed, starting at this point) introduce the key question for investigation (e.g. "What was the most important cause of the Spanish Civil War?"). Provide students with a timeline of events. They then have to tick the appropriate column to indicate which category the event fits into. Such columns might indicate positive or negative developments for the stability of the regime. If students are working on a word processor they can simply cut and paste the event into the appropriate column.

Next, students can highlight different events in different colours according to a key (for example, social, economic and military factors) and explain their reasoning for placing the event in that particular column in that particular colour. Finally, students consider the key turning points in the narrative and chunk the timeline into appropriate titled chapters. This is a useful way of helping students to see the bigger picture.

Causes of the Spanish Civil War: Overview Timeline

Task 1

Each of the events listed in this table belongs in either the left hand ("Positives") column or the right hand ("Negatives") column. Your job is to
(a) CUT and PASTE each event into the second column if it needs to be moved;
(b) HIGHLIGHT different events into the appropriate colour using the following key:

Socio-Economic	Religious	Military	Regional

NOTE: different parts of the same sentence may be highlighted in different colours.
NOTE: The events up to 1921 have been done for you.

Date	Positives for Spain: signs of stability, success, improvement	Negatives for Spain: signs of instability, failure, decline (EXPLAIN AS NECESSARY)
The Monarchy		
1851		**Religiously**, the Catholic Church had a stranglehold over education since the 1851 Concordat. This was dangerous since Church support could not be relied upon and this would offend the large minority of non-Catholics and anticlericals in Spain.
1898		**Militarily**, the army was overstaffed and overpowerful after the loss of Cuba in 1898. This was a source of instability as the army now lacked a role and increasingly looked for activity within Spain's own borders.
1909		**Socially**, problems of poverty for the peasantry and the proletariat had led to bloodshed in "Tragic Week" (1909). This created a situation where the proletariat increasingly saw the government as being against their interests.
1920		**Regionally**, Catalonia and the Basque region wanted independence. The refusal of the monarchy to countenance devolution meant that these regions remained disaffected with the government – increasingly so as they became the industrial

Categorised and colour-coded timeline on the Spanish Civil War

5. How do we measure/prove this?

Many of the points in the timeline will require substantiation. In the example relating to the causes of the Spanish Civil War shown above, the statement is made that "The army was overstaffed and powerful". But how do we prove this? How can this be measured? Students should identify as many of these statements as possible, turn them into questions for research ("How do we measure whether the army was overstaffed?") and then set about finding the answer. This is particularly valuable to teach students the importance of substantiating their arguments. It also helps students formulate proper questions for research, in a form that cannot be answered by a straightforward 'Google Search'.

6. What questions does this timeline raise that require further research?

To lead students into an independent research activity, discuss the sorts of questions that the timeline leaves unanswered. These can be in the form of "describe" (what, who, where, when), "explain" (why?) and "assess" (to what extent?).

7. Add captioned images and extra points from the video clips for key points in the story

In the lesson from which the following image is taken, students read through the first part of the timeline together, watch a short video clip from a documentary covering this period. They then make extra notes and added an appropriate image alongside each event. In this instance, this was leading towards students making a video documentary of their own.

What were the main causes of the American Civil War?
Your Task: To Create a Video Documentary on the Causes of the Civil War

Task 1: Gathering the material for your documentary

1. As a class, **read** through the first batch events in the timeline overleaf, and then **watch** the first video clip carefully at the suggested point (TIP: note carefully how Ken Burns uses music, silence, gentle panning of images, changes in the narrative voice and a focus on personal stories to generate interest and emotion).

2. Next, find BOTH a picture AND an extra point of information about each of the events so far described. In this way you will be building up the raw material for your video documentary.

3. Repeat this process (reading, watching, research and note-taking) for the rest of the timeline.

Discussion Point: At what point did the civil war become inevitable?

Date	Event	Picture	Extra points of information from the video clip / web research
1776	In 1776, the **American Declaration of Independence** united all the separate states of America. It said each state in "The United States" could decide whether to allow slavery. Half the states became "slave" states, the other half became "free" states.	JOIN, or DIE.	
1780	The "slave" states were based around the **cotton plantations** of the south. The "free" states were based around the **factories** of the north.		
1790	The "slave" states wanted the US government to respect the customs of each state (a loose "**Confederacy**"). The "free" states wanted the US government to forge a national identity (a tight "**Union**").		
Video Clip "1" from Episode 1 of Ken Burns			
1793	The invention of a new machine, the "**Cotton Gin**", made the cotton plantations in the South very profitable. As the cotton plantations grew, so did the number of slaves – and their conditions became increasingly unpleasant.		
1820	The "**Missouri Compromise**", kept a voting balance of a slave state (Missouri) and a free		

Opening section of the timeline on the American Civil War

Character cards

Providing each student with a character card at different points in a historical study is a great way to engage the class with the motives of individuals and the nature and extent of change and continuity.

Method 1: Using "before" role cards to anticipate how key characters will react to circumstances

Before studying a key moment or event in history, give the class a list of the main characters involved and encourage students to consider such things as what they might believe, say and do (or what they anticipate they will gain or lose) as the story unfolds. These could be delivered as role-play presentations or imagined dialogues.

As a result of this initial activity, students will study the event in question with a much greater interest in how different people and groups were actually involved, and will be much more engaged in discussing such things as who had the most effective reactions, whose beliefs changed the most, whose reputation was enhanced or tarnished, or whatever other issues are pertinent for the topic in question.

Case study: The Little Rock Nine

When studying the desegregation of American schools in the 1950s, the case of Little Rock in Arkansas is an essential case study. In 1957, nine black students were enrolled in the school, and this sparked off riots.

After doing the necessary background reading which enabled me to identify the key characters and how they fitted into the story, I was able to provide each of my students with a different role corresponding to different key characters involved, as shown overleaf:

The Little Rock 9: Role play / Anticipation Task

You are: Governor Faubus of Arkansas. The local school board has made you aware that nine students will be admitted early next week and they have asked you to make a statement to the press outlining your position and how you are preparing for this. You are a relative moderate, but you are aware that many of your voters have deep misgivings. What will you say?

You are: President Eisenhower. You are aware that the tension in the South is explosive and that the Little Rock situation could easily escalate into violence. You are also aware that the world's media will be focused on you. Describe how you expect things could unfold and how you will react to various scenarios.

You are: The father of a black student who has been selected – due to his/her excellent grades – to be one of 9 students to attend Little Rock High School. Try to persuade your wife that your child should take up the offer.

You are: The mother of a black student who has been selected – due to his/her excellent grades – to be one of 9 students to attend Little Rock High School. Try to persuade your husband that your child should not take up the offer.

You are: A student who has decided to take up the offer to go to Little Rock. Explain why you have chosen to do so.

You are: The leading member of the National Guard outside Little Rock School. A number of the black students have made their way into the building, but a mob is now gathering outside. What will you do to bring the situation under control and prevent it escalating further?

You are: Elizabeth Eckford, one of the black students. It is the first day of school at Little Rock. Due to a misunderstanding, you find yourself separated from the rest of the group and in the middle of an aggressive white mob. What do you do?

You are: A white student at Little Rock High. A journalist has asked for your opinion of the situation: (Who is to blame? Do you think the schools can and should be integrated?) What is your reply?

You are: Minniejean Brown, one of the black students. You have now been at the school for several weeks. You are standing in the lunch queue and you are being continually insulted, taunted and bullied by a fellow (white) student behind you. What (if anything) do you do?

You are: Ernest Green, one of the black students. You have finally graduated from Little Rock, but in the graduation ceremony you are confronted by a sea of hostile faces when you take your seat. What do you do, and what is your attitude, when your name is called out and you are expected to walk up to the stage to receive your diploma?

Role cards for the Little Rock case study

After students had delivered their presentations and we had discussed issues arising, they then watched the extract from the classic "Eyes on the Prize"

TV documentary to make notes on how events actually unfolded and how each character actually reacted and was affected. By speculating and anticipating in advance, students were much more interested and much more engaged in the discussion that followed ("Do the cases of Minnijean Brown, Ernest Green and Melba Petillo suggest that the Little Rock campaign was regarded as successful by the children involved?", "How effectively did you think (a) President Eisenhower and (b) Governor Faubus dealt with the situation at Little Rock?" and so on).

Method 2: Using "before" and "after" role cards to study the nature and impact of change and continuity

Step 1: At the start of the unit

Another simple way to use role cards in the classroom is to produce pairs of cards for key individuals from different walks of life. The "before" card is provided to each student at the outset of a dramatic period of study (for example, Nazi Germany 1933-39, World War One 1914-1918, The Black Death 1347-1350). This first card outlines, in a first-person narrative, such things as his/her situation, beliefs, hopes and concerns at the start of the period. These may be real individuals or represent generic types.

The first student reads out their character card, and the rest of the class notes down whether the character appears to be doing well in the current circumstances, and whether they are hopeful for the future. Based on the answers to these questions, the name of the character is then placed into a matrix grid (page 82) based on these two criteria, or a debate takes place about where they should be placed in this grid using a game of 'Interpretation Battleships' (page 83). The process is repeated for the remaining characters, and then students then use the completed matrix grid to reflect on the overall situation on the eve of the event in question.

Step 2: At the end of the unit

At the end of the study, each student is provided with the "after" card for their character, which outlines how the character's life and outlook has been affected over the course of the period in question. For example, some people will have become more optimistic; some more pessimistic; some will have found their situation has improved, got worse, or stayed the same; some will find that their attitudes on key issues will have changed. General conclusions and comparisons can then be drawn and key questions can start to be addressed ("To what extent did World War One lead to a social revolution?", "Who gained, and who lost, from Hitler's rule in Germany before World War Two?").

Using maps effectively

Maps can provide the basis of some very effective and interesting classroom activities. The following methods for the history classroom are transferable to other topics and subjects.

1. Convert a narrative into a Google Earth Tour

Students can be provided with a timeline of key events, and challenged to plot these on a map or in Google Earth to give them a fresh perspective and gain some geographical awareness of the topic in question. For example, I have designed such a tour to teach students about Tsarist Russia on the Eve of World War One. It is illustrated with original colour photographs from the Prokudin-Gorskii archives, organised around six groups of issues: political, economic, social, military and religious.

2. Place one map inside another to stress the scale of territory or impact

It is easy for students to overlook the vast scale of a territory being studied, despite the fact that in some instances this provides a crucial means of understanding the process of change and continuity. In this sense, placing one feature inside another can provide a quick but effective means of illustrating scale. For example:
- Provide students with a map of their own country (e.g. Great Britain). Then provide students with a map of imperial Russia. Ask them to draw a rectangle inside it somewhere to indicate the size of Great Britain. Then, provide students with an actual scaled map of Britain. Is it smaller than expected (likely)? What challenges would this provide to a ruler? A simpler method is to get students to guess how many kilometres are represent per centimetre before telling them the correct figure.
- Provide students with a map of their own locality. Ask them to draw around this the borders of another region, city, battle-lines or event. Then they should compare this to the reality. For example, students

could overlay a map showing the impact of the atomic bombs dropped on Japan onto their own locality to bring home the scale of destruction.

- Provide student with a 'then and now' overlay to demonstrate the scale of change or impact. For example, when studying World War One, I use a Google Earth Tour to zoom in on the area corresponding today to the Western Front. I ask students to anticipate where, and how many, allied graveyards can be found in this area. Then, I tick the box which reveals a folder of placemarks showing each cemetery as a small white cross. It is an absolute blizzard and generates an audible sharp intake of breath around the class. It's a very simple, but profoundly moving, map-based starter activity.

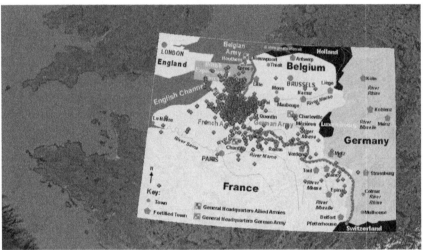

A Google Earth visualisation of Commonwealth war cemeteries on the Western Front

3. Anticipate and research key features on a blank outline map at the start of the topic

Rather than providing students with a detailed map as a reference resource - which, more likely than not, will end up filed away and neglected - give students a blank outline map and challenge them to label key cities, borders and natural features using whatever sources they can find. This is particularly useful when the study of the topic will require frequent reference to particular regions, cities and natural features.

Stage 1: Anticipation
This phase is particularly useful if students have studied this place before.

Provide students with a blank outline map and then ask them, from their existing knowledge and through their own powers of deduction, where they anticipate certain borders and places are located. Some examples might be:

- "Here is a map of Europe in 1914. Draw a line to represent where you think the Western Front started and ended by Christmas 1914"
- "Here is a map of Austro-Hungary at the end of World War One with the national minorities highlighted. Divide the territory into new states (Hungary, Austria, Czechoslovakia, Yugoslavia…)"
- "Here is a map of Germany after World War Two. Label the location of Berlin, then draw the anticipated borders of the French, British, Soviet and US zones of occupation based on what you know about the Soviet occupation and the debates at Yalta and Potsdam"

Stage 2: Research
Students should start by comparing their maps with a partner and as a class (the teacher could even try to reach a class consensus on a final, whole-class map). Then, when they conduct their research to complete a master copy, they will be much more engaged in the process and willing to answer such questions as "Were the borders substantially larger or smaller than you expected?".

If the topic is a new one, it is unlikely that the anticipation stage will be worthwhile and so students could proceed straight to this research phase. For example, I start my study of the Spanish Civil War with a homework exercise in which students are challenged to label an outline map of the Iberian peninsula with key features, cities and regions (in particular, noting where separatist movements were particularly strong, and the north-south divide in terms of agriculture and industry).

4. Use classroom debate to decide upon the most appropriate / likely border changes partway through a topic

This technique is similar to the anticipation exercise outlined above, but lends itself particularly well to topics involving debate between different parties about the most appropriate border changes. Students are arranged into small teams, with each person representing a different interest group, and they are then challenged to agree upon the fairest possible division of territory. For example:
- Provide students with a map of Palestine after World War Two. Key geographical features should be labelled in terms of population

distribution, water sources and fertile land. In teams of three (representing Arabs, Jews and the Western powers), students have to divide the territory into three areas (Palestine, Israel and International Zones) in a way which they think is most likely to bring lasting peace to the region. You should stress that you will cast a vote in favour of the best plan. Therefore, although students should aim to defend their interest group's objectives, they should be aware that being too greedy will likely mean that their plan will be thrown out altogether as being too controversial. At the end of this particular exercise, students can compare their maps to the various genuine proposals put forward before and after World War Two by the British and by the UN and discuss the merits of each.

• Another topic which lends itself well to this approach are the negotiations at Versailles (1918) and Yalta/Potsdam (1944-45) about the future of Germany. If there is time, a 'compare and contrast' exercise based on Germany's treatment after both World Wars is particularly valuable.

5. Plot the movement of individuals along a path

This approach is useful when charting the journey of a particular person over time. As an added challenge, students could be provided with a jumbled timeline and reconstruct it into the correct order by plotting the places mentioned on a map and thereby deducing the most likely order in which they happened. Google Earth is particularly effective for creating these tours, and I have created several which can be freely downloaded from www.activehistory.co.uk. Possible topics might include:

  • The circumnavigation of Sir Francis Drake
  • The Long March of Mao Zedong
  • The voyages of Marco Polo
  • The invasion of Russia by Napoleon's armies
  • The journeys of Olaudah Equiano
  • Medieval pilgrimage routes

6. Chart the expansion/contraction of an idea, an empire or a catastrophe

a. Empires
The growth and decline of Empires lends itself well to map work. Students should shade different territories in different colours to represent the

different time periods that they were absorbed into the Empire. For added challenge:

- Provide students with a timeline listing when various territories were incorporated, but don't label these on the map itself: instead, students have to identify where these territories are themselves before drawing the borders on the map and shading them in.
- Ensure that students are provided with follow-up questions to reflect upon so it doesn't become a meaningless colouring-in exercise: for example "Which was the period of greatest expansion?", "Can you find out who was Emperor at this time?", "Why did the empire not expand any further?", "What benefits and drawbacks would continued expansion bring?"

b. Diseases and Ideas

The spread of a pandemic like The Black Death can be charted on a map very effectively. Data exists for the time when the disease was first and last recorded in various cities all over Europe, and plotting this information on a map in various colours to represent various dates is an enlightening exercise when trying to get students to appreciate the scale and speed of how the disease spread.

c. Crime – geographic profiling

Geographic profiling is an activity I use when studying Jack the Ripper at www.activehistory.co.uk. It is the name we give to the technique used by the police to work out where a killer might live. It is usually the case that

- The murders will be committed close to home (to allow a quick 'return to base') and
- The murders will take place increasingly close to home as the police step up their presence in the area.

With this in mind, I instruct students to plot the location of each murder on the map. Then, based on the information, students are asked to speculate where they think that the murderer is most likely to live and to shade this area on the map. Finally, we look at what the most recent 'Ripperologists' have concluded before discussing the limitations of this evidence.

History mysteries

These investigations are designed as stand-alone projects lasting three to four hours. They teach skills of deductive reasoning, independent research, group work and structured writing.

My students complete at least one mystery project each year. Because the mark scheme stays the same, they provide a particularly useful way of measuring student progress over time. More importantly, they start each year's studies with a sharp and interesting focus.

Stage 1: The role-play

The first part of the History Mystery consists of a role-play element led by the teacher, usually involving some props. This is deliberately designed to pique the curiosity of the students. The role card for the "Iceman mystery" which the Geography and History departments use as a secondary school induction project looks like this:

Role Card Starter Activity

Cast: Teacher

Props: "Crime Scene" tape. A blanket, covering up something which is as much like the shape of a body as possible. A full-body white overall to be worn by the teacher.

The teacher should have the 'body' covered with a blanket before students get to the room. Crime Scene Tape should be placed across the classroom door. The teacher should be wearing the white coat and be carrying a clipboard to look officious. When the students are lined up outside the class, outline that over the next few lessons they will be investigating a genuine mystery. They will need to use detective skills to form their own conclusions.

Cut the tape away and instruct them to sit down away from the 'body'.

1. Point out the body to the students. Students then have to come up with a series of questions in the WHO / WHY / WHEN / WHERE / WHAT format. Write each of these into the record grid as outlined in the teacher lesson plan.

2. With the initial questions now outlined, draw a line halfway down the board underneath the questions. This is where we will start listing some 'answers'. Ask the students to hypothesize the answers to the questions as far as possible (some answers will be impossible as we have no evidence yet).

Based on this initial introductory role-play, the class is then invited to come up with a series of preliminary questions for investigation (e.g. "Who is this?", "Why did they...?", "When did...?", "What is...?", "Where are we?"). In the case of the "Iceman mystery", the questions that students came up with as a starting point included the following:

- Are we at the scene of a murder, or an accident?
- How did this person die?
- Was this person pushed or did they jump?
- Was the victim a child (the body seems very small)?
- Are we high up? On a balcony? In the forest? On a rooftop?

Investigators Tarr and Podbury introduce the 'iceman' mystery to new secondary students

Stage 2: The images

The next part of the investigation involves showing the students a series of images on the whiteboard. Each image helps the students to formulate fresh questions, amend existing ones or even form some provisional answers.

Stage 3: Deciding upon the five key questions

On scrap paper, students work individually to identify what they think are the five "Big Questions" that require further investigation. Note: some of these questions may be taken directly from the list; it is more likely though that students will form broader questions which aim to encompass several "mini-questions" from the list.

The teacher then leads a classroom discussion to gather a list of 'big questions' and to narrow these down to what we consider to be the most popular five questions overall.

The students then write these five questions down in their sheets. They should also write a provisional answer against each one to reflect what they think is currently the most likely answer.

During this times the teacher can be cutting up the evidence slips ready for the next part of the investigation.

Stage 4: The information slips

This question formulation and resolution process then continues with a series of information slips shared amongst the class. One slip is handed out to each student and they use this to come up with a fresh question or (even better) to provide a possible answer to one of the "five big questions".

There are lots of these slips, so students who work more quickly than others can be given a second or even a third slip. Once all the slips have been handed out and analysed in this way, the students are put into groups to compare their findings.

I then use the jigsaw group approach (page 95) after this feedback phase: in other words, I create a new set of groups, with each new group containing one member from each of the old groups. The feedback phase is then repeated. In this way, every single slip has the opportunity to be discussed. This is usually a very lively phase and contains quite a few 'Eureka!' moments.

Stage 5: Individual research and write-up phase

Finally, each student produces a written report which is graded against a standardised mark scheme. Specific credit is given to students who demonstrate evidence of independent research: to this end, the teacher could construct a QR treasure hunt (page 28) to accompany the exercise for students to complete at break times.

Sweets to measure change over time

Any topic that focuses on changing fortunes over time could adopt this approach, which uses a large bag of sweets to represent a key theme being measured (for example, success or satisfaction).

A selection of students sit at the front of the class to represent different individuals or themes. The rest of the class decides how many sweets they should have at the start of the time period in question. Then a series of events is read out. For each one, a different member of the class is called upon to decide who gained and who lost out as a result, and redistribute, take away or provide more sweets to the appropriate characters after discussion and agreement.

A log should be kept (e.g. in an Excel spreadsheet) of the sweets held by each person as the simulation proceeds. At the end of the simulation, the sweets should be shared among the group. Students can be asked to spot the most important turning points for different groups and to produce an annotated infographic explaining the most pertinent points.

Possible examples

Rule of Mao - sweets represent 'satisfaction' (of groups in China such as women, children, factory workers).

Rise of Hitler - sweets represent 'support' (of groups and individuals from 1929 onwards for the Nazi party).

Causes of Spanish Civil War - sweets represent 'stability' (in different areas such as politics, economics, religion).

Consequences of World War One - sweets represent 'success' (for different themes such as medicine, technology, workers' rights). Each one of these people as a homework exercise has to explain why they gained, and why somebody else lost, as a result of World War One. In the lesson, these presentations / debates can take place before the rest of the class, acting as judges, allocate out the sweets. For added sophistication, the presentations could take place in three phases: (a) short-term effects; (b) mid-term effects; (c) long-term effects.

Case study: The rise of Stalin

Five students take the role of key members of the Politburo at the end of 1922 who could feasibly have taken power after Lenin's death (Stalin, Trotsky, Bukharin, Kamenev and Zinoviev). Prior to the lesson each one prepares a short speech explaining why they are the best person to lead the Soviet Union. In the lesson, the five candidates sit at the front of the class whilst the rest of the students form the audience. A large bag of sweets is split between the audience members and then the five campaign speeches are delivered as persuasively as possible.

When the speeches are over, each member of the audience splits his or her sweets between the candidates in proportions to reflect the respective political strength of each individual, explaining their reasoning to the rest of the class as they do so. Each candidate counts the sweets they have and we record this in a spreadsheet. Then, the teacher outlines the first key event that takes place: Lenin's funeral, and in particular Trotsky's failure to attend and Stalin delivering the funeral oration. Discuss whose reputation will clearly benefit from this, and whose will suffer, after looking more closely at the details behind these developments in the form of primary source readings. After discussion, one student is nominated to decide who should lose sweets, how many they should lose, and who should gain them.

The new numbers are added into the spreadsheet along with an explanation. This process is repeated to cover subsequent key events until Stalin is left in an unassailable position in 1929. The students then convert the spreadsheet into a graph to spot the key turning points, and categorise the key causes for Stalin's rise to provide the basis of an essay.

A graph to show the shift in power over time of several Politburo members

Hexagon learning

The hexagon approach involves providing students with key pieces of information on hexagons. Their job is to organise these into categories of their choice, with hexagons being placed adjacent to each other to highlight links between them.

These groups are then glued down onto sugar paper and then the diagram is developed with titles being written over each category, and arrows being used to connect the different categories and thereby chart a 'path' through the diagram. The annotations over these arrows ultimately provide the opening topic sentences for each paragraph in the essay that will be the concrete outcome of the activity.

Case study: The rise of Stalin

How Stalin was able to emerge as leader of the USSR against apparently overwhelming odds is one of the most intriguing questions in history. In the years that following the Bolshevik Revolution, due to a series of blunders and miscalculations, Stalin had lost the support of the party leadership: so much so that on his deathbed, Lenin dictated a formal 'Testament' describing Stalin as a liability who needed to be removed from his post. He was also hated by Lenin's closest ally, Leon Trotsky, who was widely expected to step into the leadership position after Lenin's death. Yet just five years later Stalin was undisputed leader of the USSR and Trotsky was in exile.

The story of how Stalin transformed his fortunes so dramatically is a great story revolving around his treachery, cunning and downright charm. But the danger of this is that the essays that are then written by students become mere narrative, storybook accounts which do little more than give a step-by-step account of the main events between 1924-1929.

After a study of the events culminating in Stalin emerging as leader of the party, I made a list of factors which could be used to explain why Stalin became dictator of the USSR. I then put these into the Hexagons Generator I have developed at www.classtools.net to create two single-page documents containing a total of 40 hexagons.

Stage 1: Selection and Categorisation

The class was divided into pairs for the activity. Each pair of students was given a copy of the first sheet of hexagons, which they cut up and started to organise on their desks into categories of their choice. This process, involving the categorisation of 20 hexagons, took about 15 minutes. Students were encouraged to come up with no more than five categories overall. They could also choose to leave some of the hexagons to one side if they were considered less important than the others.

We then spent five minutes comparing the different categories that students had identified. Each pair of students took turns to suggest one idea for a category heading until all the ideas had been shared.

Following this, I gave each students a blank sheet of hexagons. The challenge was to identify other factors which could help to explain Stalin's rise to power and write these directly into the hexagons. After five minutes, each pair of students took it in turns to suggest an idea. If this was a valid (and fresh) idea, then the other students copied it into their pair's version of the sheet, and the students who shared the idea were each given a sweet - we had a bag of these left over as a result of our 'Rise of Stalin through sweet-eating' lesson (page 21) which had preceded this lesson! This process was repeated until the students had run out of ideas.

Each pair of students then cut up this new sheet of factors and used them to develop their existing diagrams. In some instances this involved merely adding fresh evidence into existing categories. Sometimes though it involved adding new categories, or amending earlier categories.

Finally, each pair of students was given the second sheet of hexagons and the process of categorisation continued.

Stage 2: Linkage and Prioritisation

By this stage, the students had decided upon the main factors to explain Stalin's rise to power, organised into key categories. Each of these categories could form the basis of a paragraph in an essay. However, it was still necessary to decide two things.

Firstly, students would need to determine the order in which to deal with the points in each paragraph. It would not be enough to simply introduce the category title, then randomly write about each piece of evidence from that group. This is where the hexagons are particularly useful. The six sides mean that factors can be placed alongside each other in various combinations to highlight connections between batches of factors within categories. After students rearranged their factors in this way, they stuck them down onto sugar paper with a glue stick. They could then write the title of each category over each batch of hexagons, and annotate around each group of hexagons to explain why they were arranged in that particular way.

Secondly, students had to decide how to connect their main categories together to create an overall thread of argument. They did this by drawing arrows between the factors and explaining their connections over them. For example:

"Economic problems > *created* > Divisions in the party > *exploited by* > Stalin's Cunning > *which contrasted with* > Opposition weakness"

Stage 3: Essay preparation

The final part of the process was to use the completed diagrams as an essay plan. I photographed each of the diagrams and shared them with the students. Their task was to use the diagrams as the basis of their essay answering "Why did Stalin become leader of the USSR?". Each paragraph was to focus on separate categories of hexagons, and the points made in each paragraph should have some logical order and flow. Moreover, the order of the paragraphs was dictated by the arrows linking the categories, with the opening sentence of each paragraph after the first one being based on the explanation over each arrow.

Concluding points

Hexagon learning steers students away from a narrative approach and into an analytical frame of mind. It helps them frame categories of analysis, build up their command of the material step-by-step. It provides them with the opportunity to easily change their initial assumptions, connect factors together both within and between categories, and give them a very effective basis of an accomplished written piece.

It is also a very simple approach that can be transferred to other topics and other curriculum subjects. All that is needed is an initial list of factors – contributed either by the teacher or the students – which can then be written into a blank hexagons template or turned into hexagons automatically using my www.classtools.net Hexagons Generator. Thereafter, all that is needed are scissors, sugar paper and a glue stick.

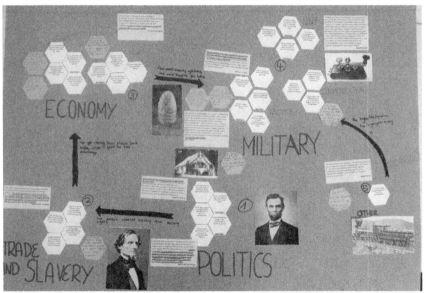

A hexagon exercise investigating why the Union won the American Civil War. Orange hexagons were added by students using additional notes from a video documentary halfway through the process. The rectangles are primary source extracts added as a final task.

Taking it further

The hexagons approach can be developed in a variety of ways, for example:

- Provide students with a blank sheet of hexagons (preferably in a different colour) and challenge them to add at least one further point in each of their categories from further research.
- Provide students with (or ask them to find) some primary source extracts (written or visual) and challenge them to add a selection of these alongside some of the categories they have developed.
- Ask students to highlight the 'most important / interesting' factor in each category and be prepared to explain their choices to the rest of the class.

The hexagon essay writing approach also overlaps effectively with the visual essay writing approach (page 126) and the sticky-note approach (page 97).

Cloze exercises

Fill the gaps, or cloze, exercises are a simple but effective strategy for helping students build up vocabulary and to learn fresh information through focused, methodical reading of a passage. They provide students with an initial blast of information prior to deeper investigation.

There are several ways to 'spice up' Cloze exercises to make them more interesting and challenging, for example:

- Don't provide students with the list of missing words straight away. Instead, challenge students to fill the gaps purely from their own background knowledge. Award extra points for anyone correctly filling in any such gaps in this 'first round'.
- If and when you provide students with a list of words that students can choose from to fill the gaps, include extra rogue words that do not appear in the text. For example:
  o Use familiar key terms from earlier topics: this is a nice way to remind students of earlier vocabulary that they have learned.
  o Use new key terms that students will learn in the topic, and then challenge students to research the meaning of each of these as an extension or homework activity.
- Don't just remove nouns – cloze exercises can also be used to help students enrich their vocabulary in other ways. For example:
  o Remove adjectives and adverbs from the account and challenge students to choose to insert the appropriate term either from their own judgment or from a suggested list. This is a particularly good strategy for developing creative writing skills.
  o Remove linking words (e.g. however, therefore, nevertheless, additionally, hence) from the start of paragraphs. This helps students think more carefully about how writers join paragraphs.
  o Remove the occasional piece of punctuation. This is a good way to get students thinking about when it is appropriate to use commas, semi-colons; hyphens - and full stops.
  o Remove entire phrases from the end of a sentence, and challenge the students to complete it appropriately.

QR code treasure hunts

A QR-Code treasure hunt involves getting students using their mobile devices to continue learning and running around outside of lesson time. A series of questions are converted into QR codes and hidden around the school. Points are awarded to students who find, decode and answer each question.

1. The background

For several lessons, the students had been engaged in a "History Mystery" exercise (page 18) focusing on the disappearance of the Franklin Expedition. Through pictures, snippets of evidence, and a role play exercise, the students formulated their own questions for investigation, framed provisional answers, and then reframed their assumptions as more evidence was progressively provided to them.

At the end of the research phase, students were required to produce an essay introducing the mystery and answering the five key questions they settled upon as being the most important to solve. The standardised mark scheme, which is provided to students in advance, gives specific credit to students who show evidence of wider research - which is where the QR code treasure hunt comes in.

2. The treasure hunt

With students just about to start their essay assignment, a series of 20 codes were hidden in random locations around the school. These were created using the www.classtools.net QR Treasure Hunt Generator.

Students were put into small teams: each of these teams contained at least one person that owned a smartphone which could decode the QR codes using one of the many free downloadable apps for this purpose.

In break times over a two-day period, the teams of students hunted around for the codes, copied down the numbered questions as each one was decoded, and then researched and recorded the answers. The completed answer sheets were then handed in at the end of the school week and the team with the most correct questions and answers was awarded a prize.

The following week, the sheets were photocopied and returned to the members of the teams. Each student could then use the fresh information they had gathered in the treasure hunt to develop their essay project in more depth.

3. Five tips for a successful treasure hunt

- Make sure the students are arranged into teams prior to the activity so that students without mobile devices are not disadvantaged.
- Make it clear that the treasure hunt will feed directly into their essay assignment and thereby help them get a good mark.
- Provide a mix of questions - some of which test existing knowledge, some of which require further independent research.
- Keep a record of where you place each code - so they can easily be removed after the exercise has finished.
- When you mark the completed sheets, award one point for each correctly copied question, and one mark for each correct answer, and declare the winning team on this basis.

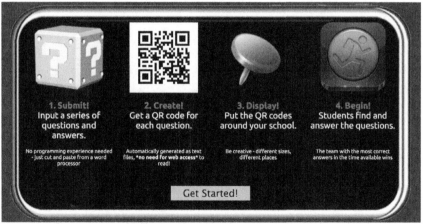

Create your own QR Treasure Hunt using the generator at www.classtools.net

Taking it further

The treasure hunt approach to learning can be developed on a larger scale across an entire locality as a local scavenger hunt (page 144).

2

DEBATE AND DISCUSSION STRATEGIES

Questions of interpretation are the lifeblood of a lively history classroom. This chapter provides useful techniques for promoting interesting classroom discussions and vigorous debates. Some of these may even be the primary method through which the topic is studied rather than merely a concluding exercise at the end of a unit.

Socratic seminars

Classroom discussions can easily end up as teacher-talk with occasional student input. The Socratic Seminar, in contrast, puts students in control, pushes teachers to the side, generates its own momentum and produces insights which might not otherwise have emerged.

Stage 1: Set the initial reading / viewing as a homework exercise

The first step is to set an initial research task as a homework exercise, along with questions for discussion, so that the students will turn up for the session ready to contribute to discussion. For example, I recently set a viewing of "Dr Strangelove" as a homework task as part of our Cold War studies, along with some questions for consideration, including:

- Did you think that President Muffley, as portrayed in the movie, provided good leadership? (TIP: Consider what defines good leadership, and whether he could have done anything better)
- Do you think the humour in the film underscores, or undermines, the serious message of the film? (TIP: Refer to a specific incident of humour in the film and to clarify the point being made)
- Based on the lessons of history, and on the conclusions we can draw from the film, what can be done about preventing the on-going threat of nuclear holocaust? (TIP: Try to find out what attempts have been made by politicians since 1945 to address this issue so that you have a specific proposal to share)

Stage 2: Conducting the Socratic Seminar

The seminar itself proceeds in the following manner.

- The class should arrange itself into a circle.
- One student will be appointed as class moderator. This student runs the activity, interjects in discussions, and keeps track of each student's participation.
- Each student should be prepared to answer the questions that formed the homework task.
- The student moderator will begin by posing the first question to the class. Anyone willing to answer should raise their hand. Nobody can speak unless called upon to do so by the moderator. The moderator should never call on a student for a second time before recognizing another student for the first time (thereby ensuring that all students' opinions may be heard).
- Students should aim to respond to points raised by other people so that the tone of the meeting becomes more of a conversation than simply a series of isolated contributions. The moderator can facilitate this by using questions like "Has anyone got any questions for X based on what they just said? Does everyone agree with X? Would anyone like to take the point made by X any further?". The moderator should also encourage contributors to explain and substantiate their points more clearly if this is necessary.
- Students may ask one of their own questions when if allowed to do so by the moderator if discussion over the previous question has faded off and the moderator allows it.
- To keep the discussion centred on the students, the teacher may only take part in discussion to clear up a factual point or to contribute an additional question.
- Students may or may not take notes as the discussion proceeds and develop their earlier answers after the session with any fresh perspectives provided by other students.

If the class is rather large, then you can arrange two circles of students, one inside the other. The inner circle conducts the seminar. The students in the outer circle must be silent and should take notes, pass on questions and provide evidence to the speakers as they occur. Pair students together so that each 'speaker' in the inner circle has one 'supporter' in the outer circle.

Balloon debates

Balloon debates start from the premise that a hot air balloon in which we are travelling is losing height rapidly. It will soon crash into the side of a mountain unless all but one person is thrown overboard. Each person on the balloon will try to persuade the class that they deserve to be saved due to their unique importance.

Lesson 1: Students research a character and prepare their presentations

In the first lesson, each student needs to choose (or will be allocated) a character relating to the topic of study - for example, eminent Victorians or the greatest women in history. Names can be allocated randomly to the students using the www.classtools.net Random Name Picker. Each student should then be given a template which they can use to frame their research:

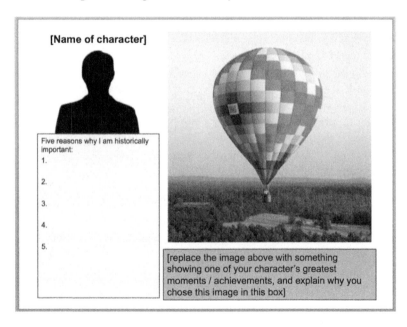

Note: Defining "Importance"
To be historically important, a person must do some or all of the following:
When?   Had an impact both in the short- and the long-term
Who?   Had an impact on a lot of people's lives
Where?   Had an impact over many countries
What?   Had an impact on many areas of life

Lesson 2: Conducting the Balloon Debate

A. Getting Ready for the First Round – focusing on 'positives'
- Give the students 10 minutes to refresh their memories and to revise the material.
- Get the presentations saved into a public area of the school network so they can be shown on the whiteboard.

B. Round one of the debate – focusing on 'positives'
- Four or five randomly selected students stand at the front of the class. The first student's presentation is displayed on the screen. The student is not allowed to read the slide – it's there only for the benefit of the audience – and they can only speak for a limited amount of time (two minutes is usually enough), explaining what they did and why they deserve to stay in the balloon.
- At the end of their speech, invite questions from the audience. These can be answered directly, or (more likely) the student concerned can nominate a 'researcher' to make a note of these questions and immediately start finding the answers to them.
- Repeat this format for the other four students.
- Go back to each of the nominated 'researchers', one after the other, to get answers to the questions raised during the debate.
- Each member of the audience then has to vote for just one character to be thrown out of the balloon.
- The two characters who get the most votes are then eliminated from the competition (more can be eliminated if you wish, depending on the size of the class and the time available).
- This process is repeated with the remaining people in the class.

C. Getting ready for the final round of the debate – focusing on 'negatives'
- Each finalist now works with a team consisting of the people they defeated in the first round of the debate.
- Their task is to gather evidence against the other finalists, for example suggesting that they were insignificant or corrupt.

- In this way, the focus of the whole debate is changed, everybody remains engaged, and the final will not merely consist of rehearsing the same old points a second time!

D. The final round of the debate – focusing on 'negatives'
- The finalists should line up at the front of the class.
- The first finalist should explain why the person to their left does not deserve to stay in the balloon. The person criticised in this way should be given a chance to respond before they in turn criticise the person to their left. The person at the end of the line should criticise the person who started the discussion.
- The audience then has to vote who should be thrown out. It is important that they don't vote for who should stay in – because there is too much of a tendency for students to vote in favour of the finalist whose team they belong to.
- The 'two hands / one hand" voting system works well here: in this format, students raise two hands (i.e. two votes against) their least favourite character, and one hand against the second least-favoured. This makes for a slightly more sophisticated voting outcome.

E. Written outcomes
As a written "outcome" you could get students to answer the questions:
- Who were the last three people to survive in the balloon, and why were they considered so important?
- How could you argue that your character was more important than any one of the three finalists?

Taking it further

- Get students to make a mask to wear during the debate. An image of the character's face, scaled up to fill the page and printed out on A4, is the ideal size.
- Students could produce a diamond 9 diagram (page 77) ranking the importance of different characters.
- Students could produce a 'Paper People' project (page 66) to connect the various characters discussed during the debate.

Silent discussion

This helps conduct close reading of detailed sources, which are placed at different points around the room. Students move between the sources in pairs, in silence, annotating with observations, questions and answers to help them answer a key question under investigation.

Stage 1: Analysing the first source

Prior to the lesson, the teacher will print off a range of sources and place them on different tables. The class will be divided into pairs, and each pair will be directed to a different table with a different source.

2 minutes: Each pair of students reads their source in silence.

3 minutes: Still in silence, students annotate their sources by underlining key phrases and either making observations, or asking questions, in the margin. Each partner can answer these questions if they wish. During this time, the teacher will move between the groups jotting down further questions and writing brief answers.

Stage 2: Moving around the other sources

All pairs will now be moved around the class to look at a different source. Repeat Stage 1 for as long as time allows. At the end of the process the teacher will lead a discussion about what has been learned. The completed sheets should be put on display where they can be compared. Students should consolidate by answering the key question for discussion.

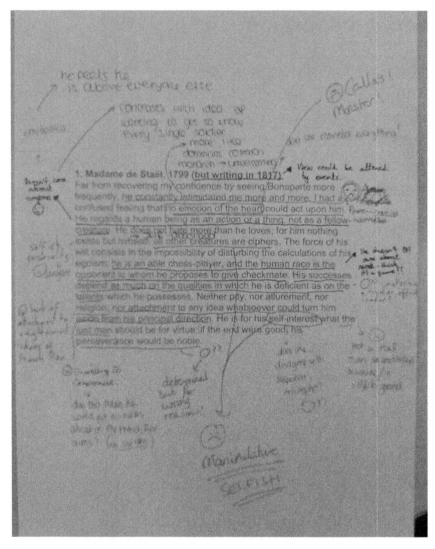

A sample "silent discussion" outcome: students move around the room annotating different sources with positive and negative observations about Napoleon, and also ask questions or make speculations about such things as the reliability of the witnesses. Subsequent students can then answer those questions and react to the earlier observations. After the exercise a discussion can take place drawing together the main observations and talking through areas of disagreement and debate.

Students as teachers, not presenters

Consider ditching the word 'presentation' in favour of 'mini-lesson'. Instead of standing passively at the front of the class reading a PowerPoint slide, each student is instead required to engage the other students in some sort of activity, task or exercise to teach the class about the topic.

I adopted this approach with my historians during their study of "What was the most significant event of the 20th Century?". The closing phase of this unit involves each student researching a topic for themselves, then traditionally turning this into an imaginary DVD documentary inlay (a template for which can be downloaded from www.tarrstoolbox.net). On this occasion, though, I asked each student instead to prepare a plan and accompanying materials for a mini-lesson lasting 10-15 minutes. I made it clear that these would be collected in and marked, and that the best five would form the basis of a one-hour lesson run by the winning students.

Taking it further

An additional bonus of this approach, which I did not immediately anticipate, is that it is a great way to get students thinking about what makes a good lesson, and the sort of thought and effort that goes into lesson preparation by their teachers. I gave the class ten minutes to discuss in groups what lessons - from any subject - particularly stuck in their memory, and why. We came up with such things as the element of competition; team work; a hands-on practical exercise; incentives and rewards; a clear outcome; and so on. The discussion was very valuable not just for the students but also for me, since it provided some great ideas about what my colleagues around the school did to engage their students in lessons which I could emulate.

Put the teacher on trial

This method motivates students to conduct vigorous research in preparation for a debate about the success or failure of a particular individual. The incentive is that the teacher will be on trial as a historical character (e.g. Henry VIII, Louis XVI, Hitler) defending his or her reputation in the 'court of history' against a prosecuting team made up of students in the class.

This trial can be conducted either as a way of revising and consolidating topic knowledge at the end of a unit, or as an intensive means of studying the topic for the very first time.

Sample motions:
- Napoleon is charged with betraying the spirit of the French Revolution
- Stalin is charged with betraying the spirit of communism
- Hitler is charged with bringing nothing but misery to his people

Stage 1: students prepare their case

Each student will be given responsibility for a particular area of policy (e.g. women's rights, economic development, religion) and should try to discover a key piece of evidence that can be used to condemn the character in question. It may be the case that several students will be allocated the same policy; in this case, they can compare their findings later and decide upon who has the strongest evidence to use in the trial.

This can then be turned into a question in the following "Is it not true that…" format:

Sample questions:
- "Herr Hitler, is it not true that your policies towards women were sexist, as proven by the fact that the League of German Maidens taught girls that their role in life was 'Kinder, Kirche, Küche'?"

- "Comrade Stalin, is it not true that your Five Year Plans betrayed communist principles, as proven by the fact that you offered cash incentives to the best workers via the Stakhanovite scheme?"

If time allows, each question should be accompanied by an 'exhibit' in the form of source material – for example a written extract, political cartoon, or statistics.

Stage 2: the teacher in the dock

Ideally, the teacher should collect in the questions prior to the lesson, and collate these in a worksheet so that students can easily take notes as the trial proceeds without having to worry about writing down each question. More to the point, it allows the teacher some time to prepare their defence!

Each student should proceed to ask their question, and the teacher should give a vigorous response to it – for example, the evidence provided by the questioner might be incomplete or unreliable. Students should take notes as appropriate.

Stage 3: the verdict

Because the students have been in full 'prosecution' mode, they are unlikely to deliver an 'innocent' verdict under any circumstances! To combat this problem, tell the students that they need to decide the charges on which the accused is least guilty. For example, if the charges focused on five different counts (e.g. religion, economics, society, politics, military affairs) then each member of the class will raise two hands for the issue where evidence of guilt appears weakest, and one hand for the second-weakest area. These votes can then be added up and the charges ranked in terms of how convincing the case against the accused appears to be. I find this works better than asking students to vote for the most guilty areas – in these cases, they inevitable vote strongly for the area they campaigned for in the trial and the results become rather predictable.

Stage 4: the judgment

Each student should conclude the exercise by producing a write-up answering the key question. For older students this will most likely be in the form of an essay.

Ditch debates, adopt arbitration

The adversarial nature of a standard debate often leads to an unsatisfactory stalemate or a simplistic declaration for or against a given motion. By moving instead to an arbitration format, students are challenged to construct a synthesis from the best points made by each side.

Overview of the traditional group debate

Classroom debates can be an effective way of getting students to think about the pros and cons of different viewpoints ("Was Hitler a planner or a gambler in foreign affairs?", "Henry VIII: Hero or Villain?"). The standard way I do this is to divide the class into two teams (the 'prosecution' and the 'defence'). Each member of each team gathers evidence for one side of the argument, then converts this into a question for their opponents ("Is it not true that…which is illustrated by the fact that…"). The best questions are then allocated to members of the opposing team at the end of the lesson, with homework time being set aside for them to formulate their rebuttals (based usually on the fact that the evidence behind the question is either incomplete or unreliable). The debate then takes place in a subsequent lesson, with the teacher acting as a chairperson and everybody busy taking notes as the debate unfolds.

Problems of this approach

The sorts of debates outline above are rigorous, engaging and thorough - but they have their limitations.

- Firstly, they can be slow to conduct (notes need to be taken by all students as the debate proceeds, which takes time).
- Secondly, the adversarial nature of a debate does not lend itself to a reasoned, synthesised conclusion – indeed, there is a danger that students could end up with the death-knell, fence-sitting judgment that "there are arguments on both sides".

The solution: arbitration, not debate

With these problems in mind, I sometimes adopt a slightly different approach which is both quicker, and more sophisticated in terms of the conclusions produced.

Step 1: Create a fresh team of 'adjudicators'

In the first lesson - the research and preparation phase - create three equally sized teams rather than just two: the prosecution and defence are now joined by a team of arbitrators. A central question like "Was Hitler a gambler or a planner in foreign affairs?" is broken down into several issues for consideration ("did Hitler's speeches suggest he was a planner rather than a gambler?", "do his actions demonstrate purpose rather than drift?", "have historians since agreed that he was a planner rather than a gambler?"). Each of these issues is allocated to a team of three people, consisting of one member of the defence, one member of the prosecution, and one adjudicator.

While the members of the defence and prosecution teams are busy gathering their evidence and formulating their questions for their allocated issue, the arbitrators are responsible for anticipating the arguments and counter-arguments on each side, and working towards a synthesis position which they hope both sides will be happy to accept (for this reason, it's best if the adjudicators are the more able members of the class).

Step 2: intimate arbitration, not open debate!

In the second lesson (the debate phase), the format of the discussion is made much more efficient by getting each team of three (prosecution, defence and adjudicator) to conduct their debates simultaneously and on separate tables. Each adjudicator listens to the questions asked by each side to the other, and to the answers provided, and makes notes. Then, with the debate element over, the adjudicator works with the pair of them to design a synthesis statement which both sides are happy to accept (e.g. "Although Hitler's speeches create an impression of drift and inconsistency, these were deliberately designed to throw up a diplomatic smokescreen around his naked ambition to ensure that the appeasers continued giving in to his demands").

In this way, with all of the issues being debated all at once and with the objective being a reasoned judgment rather than the mere 'victory' of one argument over another, the process is not only made much more efficient, but much more intellectually sophisticated.

Step 3: The adjudicators confer and conclude

In the closing phase of the process, which usually takes place in a third and final lesson after the adjudicators have polished their judgments, all of the adjudicators sit around one central table and start talking through their findings one by one, with the teacher acting as a chairperson. The rest of the class are not allowed to speak, but should make detailed notes from what each adjudicator says about what the thesis made by the prosecution, the antithesis made by the defence, and the synthesis reached thereafter.

Each of these discussions should take no more than a few minutes. If any member of the rest of the class wishes to contribute, they are only permitted to do so by passing a note to the adjudicator who was in their original team of three.

Taking it further

This approach could be used as an alternative or a follow-up to a balloon debate (page 34). Instead of the objective being to find an overall winner in a balloon debate (for example, on 'Who was the greatest figure of the Industrial Revolution?'), teams of three people could sit around a table and find try a statement which acknowledges how all deserve to be regarded as winners but in different ways ("In the short term…but in the longer term…and for women especially…").

3
TRANSFORMING AND APPLYING KNOWLEDGE

Raw historical knowledge is more effectively embedded in the memory when students apply and transform it into a personalised outcome. In its most traditional form this might take the form of an essay, but there are many other approaches that can be adopted instead or in addition.

Design a children's storybook

After studying a complex topic, challenge students to turn it into an illustrated storybook that could be understood by much younger students. Spend time in class talking through the main concepts, events and personalities that should be covered in a brief story. Consider too which images and metaphors could be used to bring the subject to life.

In themselves these books can be useful revision aids, and can be peer-assessed. Even better, arrange to read them to students in a local primary school.

Example 1: Mr. Men books: How did Hitler become Chancellor of Germany?

After completing a detailed investigation of the causes of Hitler's rise to power, secondary school students produce a 'Mr. Men' storybook which they read to primary school students. The primary students have an accompanying worksheet where their teams get points for correctly interpreting the different metaphors and identifying the key characters correctly.

A. Prior to the Activity
Pre-activity preparation for the older students
Prior to this activity, secondary students should have finished studying the Rise of Hitler. They should then spend classroom time discussing in pairs and groups how they could transform the narrative into a 'Mr. Men' story that younger students would be able to understand.
The following steps are a useful framework:
Brainstorm the key people involved (Hitler, Hindenburg, Goering, Van der Lubbe, Rohm...). Discuss their personalities / actions in relation to the topic. Bring up a picture of the Mr. Men characters on the board. Discuss which characters are the best match.
Brainstorm the key events that took place (Backstairs Intrigue, Reichstag Fire, Night of the Long Knives, Army's oath of loyalty...).

Discuss how these could be turned into analogies that would fit into a Mr. Man format. At this point it is a good idea to watch one of the original Mr. Men cartoons (easily located on YouTube or purchasable online as a DVD) to get them thinking along the right lines.

Pre-activity preparation for the younger students

Primary students should have spent some time (at least an hour or two) working through the tasks and ideas in a preparatory worksheet which provides them with essential background knowledge.

B. The Activity
Setting up the class

Primary students will be divided into groups. These teams are lettered (e.g. A-G) for easy identification and a 'team leader' is nominated within each team.

On each table, place a piece of paper which will serve as a scorecard.

The older students form a 'queue' of storytellers. The person at the start of the queue should go to Team A, the second to Team B, and so on until each team has a storyteller with it. The remaining storytellers remain waiting in the queue.

The First Story

Each group listens to the story read to them by the storyteller. Each team is then asked by the storyteller to guess what the various events / Mr. Men characters represented in real life. The team GAINS a point for each correct statement they make ("We think that X in the story represents Y"). They LOSE a point for each incorrect guess.

To keep it simple, only the 'team leader' can officially make these statements (but they can discuss with the team first). Using the scorecard on the table, the 'reader' keeps a log of how many points were gained and lost overall by each team.

Subsequent Stories

When a primary school team has finished with their storyteller, the storyteller goes to the back of the queue of storytellers. The person at the front of this queue then joins this younger team so they get to hear this new story in the same format. The process continues for the time available, or until all the stories have been read to all the groups.

Close the lesson by asking the younger students which books they enjoyed most and which readers they found read the best. Scores for the teams should be added up overnight and passed back to the older students later.

Students reading their Mr. Men books about the rise of Hitler

Example 2: Henry VIII – Hero or Villain?

In this exercise, secondary school historians produce biased storybooks about Henry VIII after completing their classroom investigations. Half the class produce books from a positive perspective, and half produce books from a negative perspective. Thought should be given to which themes should form the chapters (for example his wives, his religion, his wars) and which images could be used to create a suitably partisan impression.

In a subsequent lesson, primary school students are arranged into groups and are told that their job is to reach their own judgment of Henry based on criteria like father, husband, friend, ruler and Christian. They will do this by hearing as many stories as they can in the time available and will then complete a Wheel of Life (page 80) to reach an overall judgment. Each student is given a clipboard and a record sheet.

The younger students then listen to the story and record their thoughts. When they are finished, the reader comes to a 'neutral zone' to show they are available for reading to another group. The group they have left is then allocated a fresh reader with a story from the opposite perspective. After 20 minutes we have feedback - students are lined up along the wall from "most positive" view of Henry to "least positive". Secondary students can then observe if they "won" the argument with the students they read to.

Design a museum exhibition

As a way of encouraging focused research, or an effective means of summarising or revising a topic, get students to curate their own museum or gallery exhibit rather than risk enduring a 'death by PowerPoint'. These can be displayed in a public area, scaled down to fit into a box or turned into a 3D virtual gallery using www.classtools.net.

One easy approach to design a museum gallery task involves providing students with a large range of images relating to the topic or period in question (for example, images relating to the British Empire). They have to imagine they are curating a museum exhibition on four separate walls. How will they categorise these images? How will they caption them? What is the 'big question' which this exhibition will help visitors to answer? (for example: "What are the main characteristics of…?" or "What were the strengths and weaknesses of …?").

As an added layer of interest, some of these images may be deliberately obscure – students should place these to one side. In a second phase of the exercise, the teacher provides caption slips which have to be matched to each image prior to further thought being given to the exhibition.

Portraits as propaganda: images of Napoleon and caption slips

I have also created an online "3D Gallery" application at www.classtools.net which allows students to design a virtual animated museum exhibition on any topic. There is also a mark scheme and help-sheet to accompany this facility to make it even simpler to use. Students have to choose their images and videos carefully: they have space for exactly ten exhibits. Each exhibit should be given a title and a description for maximum educational effect. When students are finished, they can save their work for future editing, and embed it into a school website to share more widely.

3D Gallery creator at www.classtools.net

A final approach is to give each student a different theme to investigate. For example, in my study of the culture of the Weimar Republic, students choose particular topics within broad categories including art, science, literature and music. Their job is to produce an exhibition panel for a museum exhibition, paying careful attention to the key points they wish to share and what images, artefacts or sounds will best accompany their work. These can then be shared with the rest of the class and are particularly useful for understanding some of the positive legacies of a regime which is too often dismissed as a complete failure.

Design a Hollywood film poster

Get students familiar with the key events and significance of a topic by conceptualising a Hollywood feature film about it. What will be the title of the film? What key events will it focus on? Which actors will take on which roles? What merchandise could tie-in with the film?

Stage 1: Start by outlining the central task

Provide students a timeline of key events or facts about the topic. Read this information as a class. This process can take place as the very first introductory lesson to the topic, or as a review and consolidation activity at the end of the study.

ADVERTISE A HOLLYWOOD BLOCKBUSTER!

- You are a Hollywood director producing a film about Martin Luther.
- You will produce a poster advertising your film, including:
- A dramatic **title** for the film
- 4 "**Screenshots**" from the film depicting the key events of his life
- **Captions** under each screenshot describing the events
- A **cast list** (who plays Luther? Charles V? Zwingli? Frederick?)
- Some quotes from the film reviewers!

Task 1

Read through the following timeline as a class. Then, working individually, circle off four events that you think will work particularly well on the cinema screen. Be prepared to explain why. After a class discussion, watch the real trailer from the 2005 film. Did they choose the same events?

1505	**Luther** is training to be a lawyer. He is caught in a thunderstorm. He falls on his knees and promises God that he will become a monk if his life is spared. He keeps his promise!
1516	Luther has his "Tower experience" – locked away studying the Bible, he reads the phrase "the righteous will live by faith". From this he decides that God is more interested in whether we have real belief ("faith") than what we do ("Good Works"). He feels that a *Vernacular* Bible (i.e. one in the language of the people) is the only way of helping people find true faith in

Sample movie poster worksheet to help students study Luther's revolt

Stage 2: Completing the movie proposal form

Students are then asked to consider the following questions:
- What will be the title and strapline of your film? (decide whether you want to depict the main character/theme as a hero or a villain. Discuss as a class some famous film titles for inspiration).

- Choose five events to focus on? (aim for different moods: drama, suspense, humour, violence, romance...)
- Choose five people from the timeline: Which famous actors would you use to play each of these characters and why?
- What sorts of reviews could you include?
- What sort of merchandise could you advertise as a 'tie-in' promotion?

Stage 3: Producing the poster

At this stage the students are ready to produce their poster. Some students might want to create an actual movie trailer if they are keen film-makers.

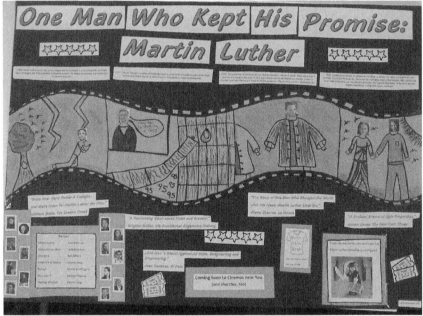

A film poster focusing on the life and significance of Martin Luther. Careful consideration was given to which characters would need to be casted, what merchandise would tie-in best with the topic, and which key events would have to be covered.

Design a memorial

At the end of a project, challenge students to design a memorial to commemorate an event, theme, topic or individual that they have studied.

Case study: Holocaust Memorial Day

Start by asking students to consider what events in international, national and personal history deserve to be 'remembered' and why (this raises the issue of how we measure significance as well as the nature of commemoration).

Then, students should be given time to research different memorials from around the world to share with the class (if time is short, the teacher could simply provide a list of these).

Next, they consider the following key questions to help them formulate their own concept for a memorial:

- What does the memorial get people to think about?
- Will it focus on the causes, or on the effects?
- Will it encourage quiet reflection, or provoke violent debate?
- What feelings does the memorial evoke?
- Regret? Guilt? Hope? Sadness? Anger? Other?
- What form does the memorial take?
- Sculpture? Mural? Gardens? Museum? Other?
- Where is it situated, and why?
- In a city (which one? why?) In the countryside (where? why?)

The final stage is to design their own memorial either on paper or as a model.

Create a social media profile

When researching a key character, students could present their findings in the form of a fake social media profile using www.classtools.net.

Using this tool, students can create a timeline of a person's life, written in the first person and in the present tense (which in itself is an effective way to prevent 'cut and paste' syndrome). They can list 'friends' in blocks on the right-hand side, and create fresh blocks for such things as 'hobbies', 'enemies' and so on. It is even possible to add video clips from YouTube. There is a 'getting started' guide and a suggested mark scheme for Fakebook projects. There is also a large gallery of sample projects to provide inspiration:

Taking it further

Fakebook walls can be created not just for individuals, but for concepts which have changed over time or between cultures (e.g. democracy, communism), to illustrate the changing relationship between countries (e.g. the developing alliance system before World War One).

Design a propaganda cartoon

Get students to design a propaganda cartoon to illustrate one key aspect of the topic from either a negative or a positive perspective. In a subsequent lesson, the cartoons are swapped around and each student answers the question "What is the message of this source?"

Stage 1: Producing the cartoon

In my studies of the Peace Treaties after World War One, I get students to design their own propaganda cartoons. Students first examine a range of famous cartoons from the period. In particular, we focus on the meaning of different symbols (the olive branch, the dove, the crocodile, the sheep) and how metaphors are made literal by cartoonists ('spineless', 'crocodile tears', 'twisting your arm' and so on).

The class is then divided into two teams: one will produce cartoons critical of the Versailles Treaty, the other will produce positive interpretations. Within each team, different students are instructed to focus on a different theme using the TRAWL memory word (Territory, Reparations, Armaments, War Guilt, League of Nations).

A final instruction is that students are not allowed to include any words in their cartoon. This will force them to focus on the visual elements rather than use words as an easy way out.

Stage 2: Analysis and Feedback

In a subsequent lesson, students swap their cartoons with somebody else in the class without any discussion or explanation. They then write an answer to the question "What is the message of this cartoon?" on a piece of paper. It is a good idea to adopt the format "I think a message of this cartoon is...the cartoonist gets this message across by showing....which I think from my background knowledge represents...".

When these answers are finished, the cartoons are put on display with the analysis for each attached underneath. The original cartoonists can then read the interpretation of their cartoon and offer their opinion on how accurately it was interpreted. Discussion can take place about how the message of the cartoons could have been improved further.

Design PlayMobil™ merchandise

PlayMobil™ recently launched a model of Martin Luther, the German Protestant reformer, complete with quill and vernacular bible. Students could design their own figure of an individual they have studied, complete with accessories.

Students could be asked to consider such things as
- What should the character be wearing?
- What should the character be holding in each hand?
- What additional merchandise could be sold as part of the set?

The first phase of the process could involve getting students to make a list of all the key characters associated with the topic, for example:
- **Origins of World War One**: Kaiser Wilhelm, Tsar Nicholas II, Franz Ferdinand, Sir Edward Grey
- **The Peace Treaties After World War One**: Wilson, Clemenceau Lloyd George and Orlando
- **International relations in the 1930s**: Stalin, Hitler, Mussolini, Chamberlain, Benes

Case Study: The rise of Hitler

When studying the reasons Hitler was appointed as Chancellor of Germany in 1933, get students away from focusing purely on Hitler's own talents and contributions by giving them different members of the Nazi party to consider, and asked them to produce a 'PlayMobil™ concept' highlighting the essential contribution of that individual to Hitler's rise, as show in the example overleaf.

Play Mobil Concept:
How Goering Helped Hitler get into Power

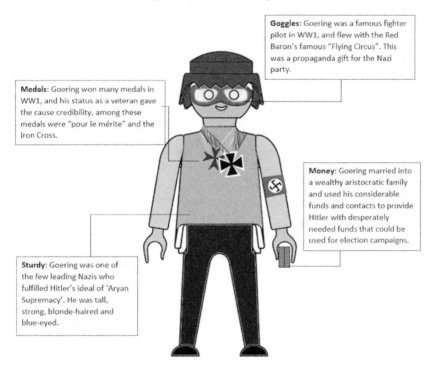

Goggles: Goering was a famous fighter pilot in WW1, and flew with the Red Baron's famous "Flying Circus". This was a propaganda gift for the Nazi party.

Medals: Goering won many medals in WW1, and his status as a veteran gave the cause credibility, among these medals were "pour le mérite" and the Iron Cross.

Money: Goering married into a wealthy aristocratic family and used his considerable funds and contacts to provide Hitler with desperately needed funds that could be used for election campaigns.

Sturdy: Goering was one of the few leading Nazis who fulfilled Hitler's ideal of 'Aryan Supremacy'. He was tall, strong, blonde-haired and blue-eyed.

PlayMobil™ concept designed to highlight individuals within the Nazi party – other than Hitler – who helped the Nazis rise to power. Note how each object is designed to help the student remember a relevant fact about how explicitly the character helped Hitler get into power.

Miming, freeze-framing, body sculptures

With younger students especially, thinking about how to physically represent what has been studied can be a useful learning experience. Thought needs to be given to what character or characters will need to be represented, what their body positions and facial expressions will be, and how they will act out the concept either in motion or as a moment frozen in time.

Freeze framing

This involves getting students, working usually in small groups, to construct a scene which is then photographed and explained. This should represent a key action moment 'frozen in time' to capture energy. It is fun to give each group something different to represent, and to keep this secret until after the scene is created for the rest of the class. In this way the other students can be challenged to guess what is being represented.

Body sculpture

This is similar to freeze framing, except in this case there is a group leader responsible (sometimes silently) for 'moulding' the rest of the group into place. These group members are not allowed to speak or move independently, they can only carry out the instructions of the team leader. This technique can also be based around paired work, with one student the 'sculptor' and another the 'clay'. After a strict time limit, the group of sculptors can then conduct a walking tour of the 'gallery', with each sculptor taking it in turns to explain their 'sculpture'.

Miming / charades

In silence, different students have to act out a key concept, event or scene. Other students gain points if they guess these correctly. For example, when investigating the power of the Medieval church, start by giving the students a list of key ways why the church was so powerful, then inform them that different students will be allocated one of the ideas at random to mime in front of the rest of the class. They then have ten minutes to consider in silence how they would act each one out. It's a great way of providing some focus to the reading.

	A. Power	B. Help	C. Fun
1	**Excommunication** is when the Pope condemns someone's soul to hell	**Confession** of your sins to a priest will help you get into heaven	**Holidays** (holy days) are days when everyone was given the day off work
2	**Courts** exist just for the Church for the trial of "sinners"	**The Mass** (bread and wine ceremony) helps people get into heaven	**Harvest Festival** is a massive party organized by the Church each year
3	**Sloth**: The Church can punish you for being lazy	**Baptism** protects young children from going to hell if they die	**Sports competitions** were organized between local churches
4	**Gluttony**: The Church can punish you for getting drunk	**Relics** (holy objects like the bones of saints) can get people into heaven	**Socialising**: Sunday Church is where people meet up and chat
5	**Envy**: The Church can punish you for being jealous of other people	**Pilgrimages** to holy places will help you get into heaven	**Music**: The choir and the church band is where people enjoy music
6	**Land**: The Church owns almost half of the land in the country	**Flagellants** say that whipping yourself will help you get into heaven	**Drama**: The church organizes plays based on stories from the bible
7	**Tithes**: Everyone has to pay taxes to the Church	**Monasteries** are places where people could devote themselves to God	**Art**: Stained glass windows and wall paintings are in the church
8	**Mortuary Fees**: The Church charges a fee to bury dead people	**Last Rites** (special prayers) are give for dying people by priests	**Reading**: The priest reads out exciting stories from the Bible each week

Miming challenges for a study of the Medieval church

Thereafter, call up a random person in the class, and secretly point out to them just one of the points from the table to mime to the rest of the group.

At the end of the mime (which should take no longer than a few seconds) each member of the class should write down in the space below the point from the table which they think it represented (e.g. "A5", "C2").

The game is repeated using 9 other students miming 9 other points, one after another. The teacher will then tell the class the correct answers and the students can add up their scores.

4

COMPARING, CONTRASTING, LINKING

When analysing the nature of cause, effect and significance, history students need to learn how to compare, contrast and link key factors to work towards an independent conclusion.

Decision trees

Decision trees are a fun and effective way to get students reflecting carefully about the similarities and differences between various factors. They work on the same principle used by questionnaires in time-killing magazines where each yes/no answer takes you down a different branch until you end up with a final answer to the central question.

Example: What is your ideal Medieval job?

When studying Medieval religious beliefs and practices, provide students with a list of activities which people in the Middle Ages thought would help them get to heaven. Explain to students that they will be acting like a careers advisor to help people decide their ideal route to paradise:

Stairway to Heaven **How will YOU get to paradise?**	
Franciscan Friar Do you like the idea of devoting your entire life to God, but still want to be able to travel around and help ordinary people at the same time? Yes?! Then the Franciscans are for you! Your job is to move around from place to place spreading the word of Jesus and helping out in the community however you can. You will have to take a vow of poverty, though, so if you like material things then you may wish to think twice!	**Pilgrim** Do you like the idea of travelling with friends to foreign lands? Have you got a spare bit of money to fund the trip? If so, the job of pilgrim is just for you! You will go to holy places like Lourdes in France, and see relics of holy people – even their mummified hands, and pieces of the cross Jesus was crucified on! By praying at these places and going on these journeys you will please God and get into heaven!
Cistercian lay brother Not too bright, but not afraid of a bit of hard physical work? Then why not become a Cistercian lay brother?! All you have to do is go along to the Cistercian Monastery and work as a gardener, a builder or a plumber. This is a great job if you fancy a quiet life - you will not be allowed to leave the monastery once you have joined up.	**Crusader** Do you like adventure? Do you like violence – even violence - your sort of thing? If so, Crusader could be just the thing for you! You will go to the Holy Land with an army of comrades to fight the Muslims who have taken over Jerusalem. It's dangerous work, and you will need a fair bit of cash to fund the enterprise, but God will be pleased with you!
Augustinian monk Do you like the idea of living in a secluded monastery away from the hustle and bustle of everyday life? Are you not too keen though on being completely out of touch with the real world? Augustinian monk is just the job for you, then! You will spend most of the day at quiet prayer, but you will also be able to provide shelter for travellers and medical care in the local community!	**Flagellant** Not too keen on travelling? Not too scared of a bit of pain? Maybe Flagellant is just the job for you! All you have to do is walk around town whipping yourself for your sins. God will be so pleased that you are punishing yourself on earth that he will let you into heaven as soon as you die.
Cistercian monk Are you bright and ambitious? Do you like the idea of a quiet life? Cistercian monk is the right path for you! You will live your life in quiet devotion to God in a monastery deep in the countryside. You will have to leave all your family and friends behind, but the peace and tranquillity – in fact, you will not be allowed to speak at all because you will take a vow of silence!	**Charity worker** Do you have bit of time and / or money to spare? Do you like the idea of helping others through the Church, without having to give up your ordinary way of life? Yes? Then why not do some "Good Works"? If you help the poor by washing their feet or giving them bread, God will be pleased! If you buy an "indulgence" from a "Pardoner", God will forgive you your sins! If you leave money to the Church when you die, you will get into heaven more quickly!

Students then produce a decision-making tree to help people decide which "stairway to heaven" most closely matches their own personality, interests and abilities. For example, one question might be "Do you like travel?". Students can draw up their findings as an A3 diagram, a mind map, or even an interactive website if they are so inclined.

The crucial tip to give students is that they should aim to design questions which divide the remaining factors into two roughly balanced "Yes" and "No" categories. This is what really gets them thinking and reading carefully.

The following template, created using the SmartArt > Hierarchy feature in Microsoft Word, gives students a useful starting point. I award extra credit to students who include illustrations and even additional jobs they research themselves to add into the project.

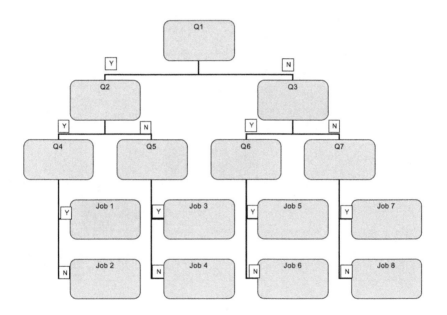

Taking it further

Get students to test their decision trees out on each other in a 'speed-dating' format. They may spot how their original questions need to be amended. Make sure that details about each answer, rather than just (in this case) the job title is included. For display pieces, a particularly effective technique here would be to have each final answer in the format of a gift card or advent calendar, where the viewer has to physically open up the card to learn more.

Linkage bingo

This whole-class game helps students to summarise issues of cause or effect, and then to link them together in a meaningful way prior to producing an essay.

The class should be divided into teams. One person in each team should be the scribe. A version of the template will be on the whiteboard ready for the teacher, as quizmaster, to fill in as the game proceeds.

	> 1. Political	> 2. Religious	> 3. Military	> 4. Regional
1. Political factors >	POLITICAL FACTORS X 3			
2. Religious >		RELIGIOUS FACTORS X 3		
3. Military >			MILITARY FACTORS X 3	
4. Regional >				REGIONAL FACTORS X 3

The template shown above, which I use to investigate the causes of the Spanish Civil War, is merely a suggestion. It can be adjusted by the teacher to list however many factors need to be considered for the issue being considered.

Example questions:
- What were the main causes of the Spanish Civil War?
- Why was Hitler able to become Chancellor of Germany?
- What were the effects of World War One?
- What was the impact of Stalin's rule on the Soviet Union?

Round 1: Revising the Factors

In this round, each team will be challenged to contribute factual points to place into one of the darkly shaded cells (randomly chosen by the teacher).

Each team gains one point for each valid, explained point they make, up to a maximum of three points.

Each team will be given five minutes preparation time to decide what they could contribute for all the cells before the round begins.

Round 2: Linking the Factors

The teacher should roll the die for each team. The number allocated to each team corresponds to the factor on the left that needs to be connected to one of the blank cells along that row. For example, if the team rolls a 'two' they need to explain how socio-economic factors led to or exacerbated one of the other factors.

The entire class will be given several minutes of team time to prepare their thoughts. Each well explained point will gain two points for the successful team and will be written into the table by the teacher.

Taking it further

- The teacher may initially roll the die twice for each group to provide both a row and a column that the team will need to complete.
- As the game proceeds and fewer cells are left blank, teams may nominate the cell they wish to complete (or nominate one for the next team).

Homework / extension tasks

When the table is complete, the game is over. The teacher will provide students with a completed copy of the record sheet. Students produce their own flowchart of the strongest links as the basis of an essay plan. They write the opening topic sentences as appropriate and discuss these with the teacher before writing the essay in full.

Paper people

To help students connect factors together in a 'chain of causation', take each individual (or personify each factor – for example, Nazi Propaganda could be personified as Goebbels) and connect them together in a paper chain.

The completed diagrams not only form the basis of a classroom display, but can also be used for essay planning: each link explained across the arms forms the 'topic sentence' of each paragraph and the 'body' of the paragraph is the 'body' of the person. This is an approach that I recall was originally shared with me by Lesley Ann McDermott (@LA_McDermott).

Here are the instructions I gave to my historians after completing their balloon debate (page 34) considering 'Who was the most significant figure of the 19th Century?':

- Highlight at least five key individuals within different categories
- Include an image of each key character as its face
- Include the name of each key character across the shoulders
- Include detail about achievements. in the body
- Include sentences summing up qualities of each person on the legs
- Establish connections between people on the arms between them

Target diagrams for categorisation

Target diagrams enable students to break down a key question into categories and subcategories. Three factors are placed in the centre of the diagram. In the next layer, each factor can then be broken into two examples. In the final layer, each of these examples can then be substantiated with factual detail / illustrative points.

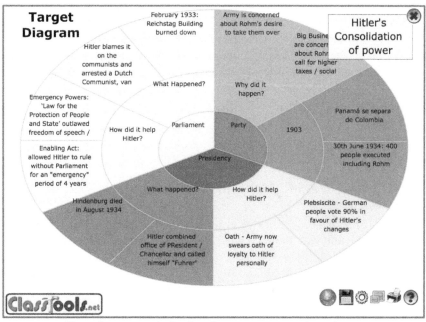

Target diagram created using the online generator at www.classtools.net

Sample lesson plan using the template

Provide students with a key question, for example "What were the effects of World War One?"

Students are asked to come up with three broad categories that could be used as the basis for the investigation, e.g. social / political / economic.

These are written into the central area.

Then, students comes up with two examples for each category. This process could be managed as follows:

- Give each student a number (1, 2 or 3) corresponding to one of the three categories.
- Each student has a few minutes to come up with two key examples to illustrate their allocated category of factor.
- All the number "1"s sit together and compare their ideas, as do the "2"s and "3"s.
- Each group decides what the two best points are to keep.

The teacher then asks each group to feedback with their findings. These are recorded in the middle layer of the diagram.

Finally, the students are asked to fill in the final layer of the diagram themselves with substantiating detail for each of the six examples now identified. They could do this in groups and feedback to the class again.

Alternatively, the teacher could save the template onto the network so that students can open it up and work on it individually, or print off copies so that they can be completed by hand.

Taking it further

- The teacher could complete one segment of the diagram (Social, Political or Economic) in advance of the lesson to give students a clearer idea of what needs to be done with the remaining two sections.
- Students could write an essay based around the key question using their template as the basis as their central three paragraphs.

Venn diagrams

A Venn diagram allows students to compare and contrast the similarities and differences between two or three key events, concepts or people.

In a Venn diagram, which usually consists of three overlapping circles, characteristics shared in common go in the central area; those shared by just two factors go in the area where those two circles overlap; characteristics possessed by just one go in the outer area of that circle where it does not overlap the others.

Stage 1: Individual work

To get started with Venn diagrams, ask students to identify three key people, events or factors they have become familiar with. In History, they could compare three different rulers or countries.

Hexagon Venn template available at www.tarrstoolbox.net

Stage 2: Group Quiz

After students have finished their individual Venn diagrams, the teacher could follow this with a team competition. rules are very simple. Once the students have completed their work, they are put into teams and have a few minutes to compare their findings and develop their diagrams.

Then, each team will be given an answer buzzer. The teacher will nominate one "Zone" of the diagram. The first person to press the buzzer can answer by providing a relevant point that fits into that section of the diagram. If they are correct, they win for their team the appropriate amount of points for their team. If they are wrong (or hesitate or repeat a idea already shared), they lose the same amount of points for their team. The quiz can continue over several rounds. The end result is that all the students end up with a detailed resource for revision purposes or for the write-up phase of the project.

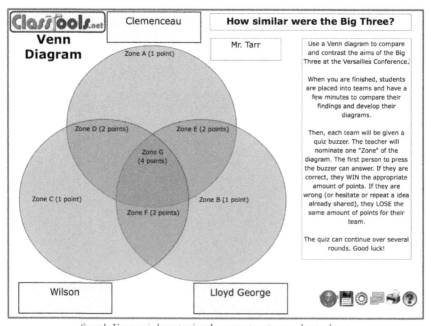

Sample Venn quiz layout using the generator at www.classtools.net

Wedding invitations and bio-poems

Provide students with two characters from their studies, spot connections between them, then design a wedding invite.

Template available at www.tarrstoolbox.net

In the example shown here, note how the students are encouraged to include specific relevant details from their studies in the poem and in the 'further information' at the bottom of the invitation.

Incorporating a bio-poem

The poem provided in the example on the previous page follows no particular format, but this would be a good opportunity to get students to create a "Bio-poem" for each character. The format is as follows:

- Line 1: First Name
- Line 2: Four descriptive traits
- Line 3: Sibling of...(or parent of / child of)
- Line 4: Cares deeply about...
- Line 4: Feels...
- Line 5: Fears...
- Line 6: Needs...
- Line 7: Gives...
- Line 8: Longs to see...
- Line 9: Resident of...
- Line 10: Last Name

Taking it further

The bio-poem format can be adapted. For example, discuss with the class what alternative openings could be used and then decide upon a common format before beginning the task. For example, here are some additional stems:

- Understands that...
- Enemy of...
- Pretends to...
- Whose lasting legacy is...
- Hero to...

The best poems could be illustrated, read out in class or recorded, and used for display purposes.

5

JUDGMENTS & INTERPRETATIONS

Through the process of linking, comparing and contrasting key factors, students are working towards an overall judgment and interpretation on the historical questions being investigated. This chapter considers methods for helping students reach and share their conclusions with their peers.

Counterfactual history

To help students decide how important a factor was in causing a particular event, ask them to consider whether events would have turned out differently without it.

To have validity, this 'counterfactual' approach should not descend into mere speculation. Instead, students should be prepared and trained to substantiate their assertions with evidence to help build a case for a given factor being a genuine cause, a mere catalyst, or downright irrelevant. It also gets students thinking about some deep questions about causation such as the intentionalist view of history (which places an emphasis on the actions of individuals) as opposed to the more deterministic structuralist interpretation (which focuses instead on the role of institutions and deep-seated conditions). From there, it is a short step to the philosophical discussion about free will versus determinism. It is also an approach which has been pursued by major historians such as Sir Richard Evans and Niall Fergusson.

Example: Why did Hitler become Chancellor of Germany?

Step 1: Review the narrative

At the end of a detailed study of the causes why Hitler became chancellor of Germany in 1933, start by presenting students with a summary of what they have learned so far as a summary digest:

> "In 1921, a final reparations sum of £6.6 billion was imposed upon the Germans. Claiming that their economy was already severely damaged by territorial losses under the Treaty of Versailles, they claimed they were unable to pay. So in early 1923 the French and the Belgians invaded the Ruhr. Strikes and demonstrations led to complete economic collapse, and the government made things worse by simply printing off more paper money to 'inflate' the economy again. The result was hyperinflation, which wiped out life savings overnight and led to a surge of support for Hitler's Nazi party. At this point, Hitler sensed an opportunity and launched his

Munich Beer Hall Putsch. This was easily crushed by the police in clashes which led to the deaths of several Nazis. However, Hitler used his subsequent trial to promote his ideas and used his prison sentence to write *Mein Kampf* and to change his strategy ("We must hold our noses and enter the Reichstag). Meanwhile, Germany superficially recovered: the USA gave Germany a series of massive loans in the Dawes Plan (1924). However, in 1929 the Wall Street Crash sent the American economy into a sharp Depression. The USA called in its loans from Germany, which threw the German economy into another crisis and which once again led to a surge in support for the Nazi party. By the end of 1932 the Nazi party was easily the largest party in Parliament (although its support was already beginning to decline as the Depression started to fade away), and President Hindenburg was persuaded by his advisors to appoint Hitler as Chancellor in a coalition government in January 1933. Hitler rapidly manipulated the situation to turn himself into a dictator. Within ten years he had unleashed World War Two, which not only destroyed Germany but which also accelerated the collapse of the British Empire, the emergence of the USSR and the USA as world superpowers, and the declaration of Israel as a safe home for the Jews following the horrors of the Holocaust."

Step 2: From narrative to analysis: identify the key factors

The next stage is to discuss with the students what appear to be the most important factors explaining Hitler's rise to power. To help with this process, different students could be encouraged to identify short-term, mid-term, and long-term factors; others might be asked to identify political, economic, or diplomatic factors. List these on the board and, if there are too many, reduce them down to the most popular (for example, by using the 'factor auction' approach).

Step 3: Construct the counterfactual

This important stage involves constructing a feasible alternative scenario to what actually occurred in relation to the each given factor. These can be provided by the teacher, or formulated in groups. For example:

- **Factor**: The 'Backstairs Intrigue' of von Papen and Hindenburg.
- **Counterfactual**: "In 1933, Hindenburg refused to appoint Hitler as Chancellor"

- **Factor**: Hitler's personal charisma.
- **Counterfactual**: "In 1923, Hitler was killed during the Munich Putsch"

Step 4: Frame the question for consideration

Next, explicitly guide the students to consider what might have happened in these counterfactual scenarios by framing a clear question for consideration ("Will the party still get into power under someone else's leadership after Hitler's death?", "Will the Nazis find it increasingly difficult to get into power due to Hindenburg's intransigence?"). These can be accompanied by more open-ended questions that can apply to all the scenarios (e.g. Does the Weimar Republic become more, or less, stable? Does the leadership and / or strategy of the Nazi Party change? Does support for the Nazis increase or decrease? Does the Nazi party take power sooner, later or not at all?).

Step 5: Reflection and feedback

Students should then be given time to consider one or more of the counterfactuals, either alone or in small groups, before sharing their findings through jigsaw groups and/or a teacher-led discussion. They could then prioritise their factors overall using a tool such as a Triangle 9 (page 77), a matrix grid (page 82) or similar.

Taking it further

When students have finished their reflections, they could rewrite and develop the original account of events provided at the start of the exercise to reflect how things would have turned out had certain "What if...?" events had really happened.

Diamond diagrams for prioritisation

Students are given (or produce) essential pieces of information which they arrange in order or significance, success or status in a diamond diagram.

Most commonly the diamond is arranged for nine factors, but they can also be for sixteen or twenty-five. In my history classroom I have used them to arrange the outcomes of the Treaty of Versailles from most successful to least successful; evidence that a particular individual deserves to be regarded as a hero or a villain; most important to least important reasons why the slave trade was abolished.

Group / display work: image-based diamond diagrams
Students can order pictures instead of text statements – for example, images which create a positive impression of a figure or period go towards the top. Each factor could be printed off on a separate sheet of A4 paper and then arranged as a group exercise. In the picture above, students researched the origins of surnames of people in the class. The ones that corresponded to jobs – e.g. Baker, Tarr, Butcher – were then arranged in a Diamond 16 diagram from highest status to lowest status. Different pairs of students came out of class to adjust the diagram after discussion until everyone had

their input. We then transferred the diagram onto a display board.

The "Triangle 9" template

Diamond templates have a lot of wasted space which could be much better deployed for including explanations and illustrations of student reasoning. With this in mind I have created a 'Triangle 9' template: it works exactly the same as a Diamond 9, but with specific areas created for students to explain clearly why they have decided to place some factors nearer the top or the bottom. You can download the Triangle 9 Template, along with Diamond 9, 16 and 25 templates, from www.tarrstoolbox.net.

Triangle 9: Title Here

Choose 9 factors to discuss. Organise them so that the most important are towards the top, and the least important towards the bottom. Explain your choices in the boxes on the right.

Title here Description here	This is the most important factor overall because…	[Image here of something to do with the most important factor] Most important ∧
Title here Description here	Title here Description here	These two factors are less important than the one above because …
Title here Description here	Title here Description here	Title here Description here
Title here Description here	Title here Description here	These two factors are more important than the one below because …
Title here Description here	This is the least important factor overall because…	[Image here of something to do with the least important factor] Least important ∨

Triangle 9 template available at www.tarrstoolbox.net

78

Continuum lines: measure opinions on one issue

Continuum lines are a simple and effective technique for providing a breakdown of a complex question.

For example, when considering the question "Did Napoleon betray the spirit of the French Revolution?", debate each key policy area using a "Teacher on Trial" format (page 40) and then conclude by organising the policies along a continuum line containing a number of gradated possibilities to end up with something like this:

Did Napoleon betray the spirit of the French Revolution?

Legal Reforms	Church	Finance/Economy	Local Gov't	Education	Propganda	Censorship	Slavery
Revolutionary?		**Reformer?**	**Consolidator?**		**Underminer?**		**Reactionary?**

The completed diagram can then be used as the basis of an essay plan, with each of the policies being dealt with from left to right.

Taking it further

Continuum lines can be combined effectively with the 'Wheel of Life' template (page 80). The policies listen in the example above (for example, education, propaganda and slavery) could form some of the main spokes of the wheel, and students can then rate each one in terms of its success.

Wheel of life

This is a simple, visual way to evaluate historical characters and events from more than one perspective.

At the end of the study, students are given a historical character to evaluate and write their name into the template.

They then decide on at least four, but up to eight, ways to rate this character (e.g. loyalty, friendliness, intelligence, determination, tolerance – this can form the basis of an interesting classroom discussion in itself).

Next, students place a dot on each line to rate the character for each of the categories (with ten being the best score).

The dots are then joined up, and the area within shaded in a bold colour, to produce the completed wheel of life.

To round off, students should provide an explanation for their diagram underneath or overleaf.

Taking it further:

- Arrange students into a continuum line (page 79), with the most positive interpretations at one end, and the most negative at the other. Ask the student at each end of the line to justify their opinion and then ask the rest of the class to swap positions if they have been persuaded that their original judgment was too harsh or lenient.
- Print off the wheels of different students and arrange them in a diamond 9 diagram (page 77) as a classroom display piece.
- Create a 'physical' wheel of life by arranging eight students on the playground – each step outwards from the centre of the circle (up to a maximum of ten) for each of the categories of analysis.

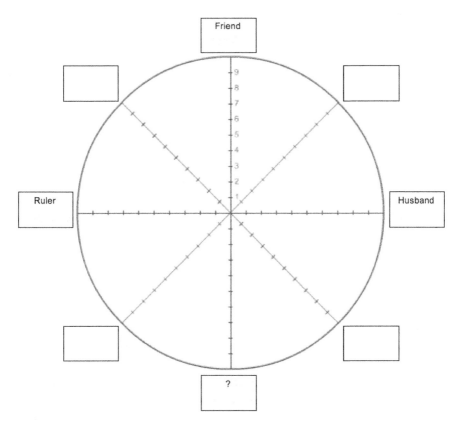

The wheel of life template can be downloaded at www.tarrstoolbox.net.
Although it most obviously lends itself to assessing key individuals, it could also be used to assess the success and failure of a regime such as the German Weimar Republic or similar.

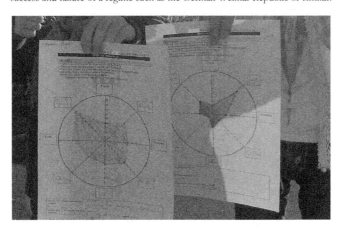

Matrix grids: judge two issues at once

It is often necessary to form a judgment on two separate but related issues. Matrix grids do this in a visually engaging way.

For example, "How successfully did Lenin rule Russia?" and "How Marxist was Lenin's regime?" are connected, but subtly different (for example, his greatest practical successes in economic terms came when he departed from strictly Marxist principles).

To highlight these differences, and to get students thinking about each one more deeply, conclude the study by dividing the board with a horizontal and a vertical line to create four squares. The vertical line represents one issue (e.g. "Success / Failure") and the horizontal the other (e.g. "Marxist / Not Marxist").

Next, consider different dimensions of the topic that can be used to reach a judgment. In the example outlined above, these would be key policy areas: the Treaty of Brest Litovsk, the Civil War, The NEP, the handling of national minorities and so on. For each one, discuss where it belongs in the diagram and then write it into that spot.

Finally, ask each student to write their own name (in a different colour) to represent their overall judgment.

The completed diagram can then form the basis of an essay consisting of four main sections corresponding to the zones of the diagram.

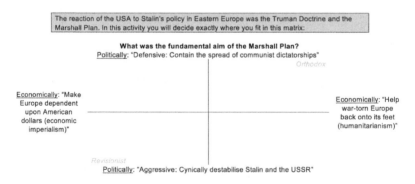

Example matrix grid: What was the aim of the Marshall Plan?

Interpretations battleships

This activity is a development of the matrix exercise, making it more sophisticated and engaging. It is a particularly effective way to get students analysing lots of information for a fresh topic.

I use this approach very effectively to teach Eisenhower's foreign policy without any prior knowledge or preparatory study.

As per the matrix format (page 82), students are given two key questions to consider (e.g. "How successful...?" and "How innovative...?") and then place particular pieces of evidence along the horizontal and vertical axes to reflect what is suggests is the correct spot with regard to each question. The vertical axis represents two opposing views on the first question (e.g. success v. failure); the horizontal axis the second (e.g. revolutionary v. reactionary). In the following example, students considered the two questions "How successful was Eisenhower's foreign policy?" and "How new was Eisenhower's 'New Look' foreign policy?".

However, the twist is to turn the whole process into a team competition called 'interpretation battleships'. This involves subdividing each quadrant of the matrix into four boxes (thereby creating 16 boxes in total). These are then individually referenced using a simple key (horizontal = letters, vertical = numbers), creating a grid of 16 squares that can be referenced as A1 to D4):

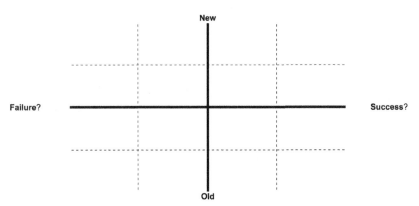

Sample grid for analysing Eisenhower's foreign policy

Phase 1: Individual research / group discussion

Each member of the class is provided with the pieces of evidence that will be considered. In the case of my lesson, this consisted of a very detailed article covering nine different policy areas, each considered under a different subheading. These policy areas are divided between three different teams. Working individually at first, then comparing their ideas with the rest of their team to reach a group agreement, students decide where their allocated policy areas and pieces of evidence belong in the matrix, and write a sentence of explanation on scrap paper ready for the game.

When they are finished with these allocated areas, they should repeat the process a second time for the remaining factors so that they have had change to consider them all. At the end of the process, each team will end up with their own version of a matrix which might look something like this:

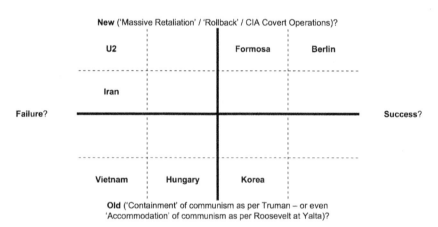

Phase 2: playing interpretation battleships

When everyone is ready, the first policy area and piece of evidence is introduced. The group who was allocated this piece of evidence (the "Quizmaster" team) stays quiet whilst the other two teams nominate the cell of the table that they think it should belong in and explain why. They should try to persuade the Quizmaster team with their reasoning.

The Quizmaster team listens carefully and then confers to decide whether they want to keep this factor in the cell they originally decided, or whether they want to adjust their decision based on the ideas they have heard.

The Quizmaster team then announces where, after full consideration, the factor belongs in the grid, and explains their choice. The teacher should record this decision in a 'class' version of the matrix.

A competing team gets one point if it placed the factor in the same quadrant as the Quizmaster team, and a further point if they placed it in exactly the same cell.

All students take notes to make sure they are clear for the reasoning behind this, and then the process is then repeated for the remaining cells of the table.

Taking it further

This approach is a really efficient way of getting through a big topic very efficiently and analytically which might otherwise involve inordinate amounts of classroom reading and teacher-led discussions.

It could be followed with a source-work exercise, where the views of key historians on the issues covered have to be organised in the matrix. This would be a very good extension or homework task for individual students to ensure that historiography was incorporated.

Each quadrant of the completed diagram can form the basis of a four-paragraph essay addressing both of the key questions covered at the start of the activity.

Write a school report on a historical character

When assessing the successes and failures of a particular historical figure, consider approaching the task in the form of a school report. This can be the basis of a consolidation exercise at the end of a topic, or an efficient way of covering fresh material.

Start by identifying the main 'subjects' that reports will be required for (e.g. economics, law, politics…) and write these down.

Discuss the successes and failures relating to the first subject. Consider how this could be written in the form of a school report ("Tsar Alexander II has had a mixed term in terms of his legal reforms…", "Adolf has been rather disruptive in his attitude to group work in recent weeks…"). Students tend to have a bit of fun recycling teacher platitudes and getting in the habit of writing a 'compliment sandwich' that starts with something positive, then makes a criticism, then closes with another positive point.

Next, provide students with an A3 version of a school report template. They then write the first report in strict timed conditions, using key words. When the time is up, repeat the process for the remaining subjects.

Taking it further

- Students should provide an effort and attainment grade for each subject as well as a written comment. This could provide the basis of an interesting discussion.
- After completing each subject report, students should swap their sheets with another member of the class. In this way, each subject report is written by a different person and looks more authentic when it returns to the original owner.
- After the exercise is completed, students should underline clear evidence of success in one colour, failure in another.

SUBJECT	GRADES		Comments
	Attainment (A-E)	Effort (1-5)	
Maths			
			Key term: Aliens; Untermenschen; Stab in the Back
History			
			Key term: Subhumans; Reichstag Fire; Treaty of Versailles; Polish Corridor
Biology			
			Key term: Aryans; Social Darwinism; Euthanasia; Sterilisation
Geography			
			Key term: Lebensraum; Alsace Lorraine
Physical Education			
			Key term: Master Race; Hitler Youth; League of German Maidens
Religious Education			
			Key Terms: Führer; German Faith Movement; Reich Church

BERLIN NAPOLA: SUMMER REPORT 1939

NAME OF STUDENT:

Form Tutor's comments:

Sample report template available at www.activehistory.co.uk. Note how it is helpful to provide students with key words within the template to help them frame their report. I get the students to pass their report sheet on to a fresh partner after each subject has been presented by the teacher and summarised by the students. In addition, any student finishing their write-up before the allocated time should underline the key words to confirm they have included them.

Triangulation: judge three factors at once

This method allows for three related interpretations to be compared visually. Write the three factors, options or interpretations on different points of a triangle. Students have to then write their initials in the appropriate spot to indicate their position.

Next, get students who are most clearly in disagreement to explain their choices to the class. Allow other members of the class to adjust their position in the triangle based on what they hear.

It is a good idea to blank out the central part of the triangle. This prevents students from defaulting at the 'fence-sitting' option of placing themselves in the middle of the triangle:

Was the Union victory in the American Civil War due to political, military or socio-economic factors? This particular example is being combined with a continuum line (page 79) to help students decide whether Confederate weakness, or Union strength, was the main cause of the war's outcome.

6

GROUP WORK APPROACHES

Many of the ideas discussed so far have a strong element of collaboration within them. Formalised group work strategies are nevertheless an important feature of the history classroom. This chapter proposes a range of particularly effective methods of getting students working together to investigate historical issues.

The Apprentice

Adapting the format of the TV show "The Apprentice" can foster group work, research and presentational abilities.

In my classroom, I use the format of the TV show "The Apprentice" to help students research and prioritise the methods used by the 19th Century Abolition Movement to outlaw the slave trade. Students are organised into teams, each one of which needs to produce a 'joined-up' campaign to abolish the slave trade. This includes choosing a target audience, a celebrity sponsor, merchandise and a publicity stunt. During the feedback phase their methods will be compared and contrasted with the actual techniques used at the time. The most impressive contributors go through to a grand final where they work with the other students to demonstrate their skills of research and presentation. After an overall winner is declared, all students are required to produce an individual project reflecting on why the slave trade was actually abolished.

Stage 1: Introduction to the task

The class is introduced to the task and is arranged into teams of 4-5 people. For the remainder of the lesson (and ideally for homework) each team has to come up with: (a) The name of their pressure group; (b) A logo and (c) A slogan.

Stage 2: Research and preparation

Lesson time is now set aside for teams to get to work on their campaign.
All teams should start by deciding upon a target market for their campaign and be prepared to explain why they think this group will be able to help abolish the slave trade. The teacher should ensure as far as possible that each team has a different target market.

Once each team has identified its target market, they will need to decide how to organise the team to decide upon the remaining aspects of the presentation:
- Location for the campaign
- Merchandise

- Celebrity sponsor (based on a real-life personality from the period)
- Publicity stunt

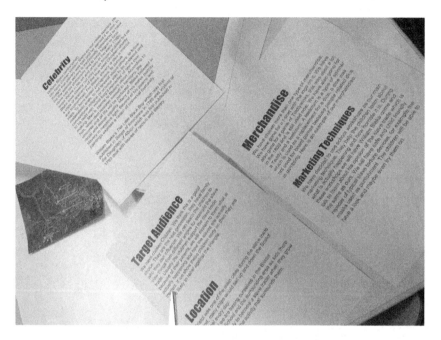

At the end of this preparation period, each team should have arranged their ideas and images onto a large piece of coloured card ready for the boardroom meeting with "Lord Sugartrader".

Taking it further:
The teacher could show the teams the series of images relating to life on the plantations (complete with captions). Each team should be allowed to nominate three of these images which they want to add into their campaign.

The teacher should then print these off and give them to each team to develop their presentations further (they will be required to justify their choices during the boardroom meeting).

The teacher could also show each team different arguments provided by pro-slavery campaigners in favour of the slave trade. For each one, the team should be challenged to reflect on how they would respond to these arguments.

Stage 3: The boardroom meeting

The teacher, in role as 'Lord Sugartrader' now proceeds to interview each team about their campaign. He starts by asking each team in turn about their pressure group name / logo / slogan and why they think it is effective. Other teams might be encouraged or instructed to make constructive criticisms about the work of other teams (to keep this positive, the question might be phrased as 'What do you think is the most effective aspect of the logo/slogan designed by Team X?").

At the end of this first round of questioning, the class should be shown some actual Abolitionist methods from the period and be invited to comment upon them in terms of their strengths and weaknesses.

This format is then repeated for the remaining aspects of the campaign (location, celebrity sponsor, merchandise, publicity stunt - using the appropriate parts from the presentation).

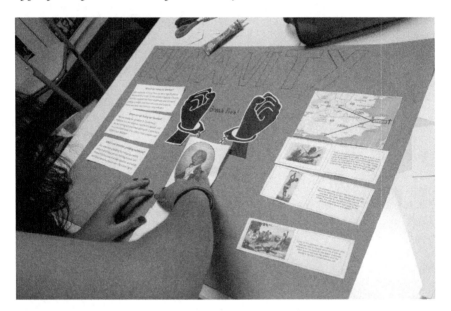

Taking it further

As part of the feedback process at this stage, the teacher could ask each team leader to answer the question "If each member of the team could be described as a body part, how would you do this?". I have written a blog post and provided a template for "What part of the body were you?" on www.tarrstoolbox.net.

At a relatively early stage, Lord Sugartrader may wish to 'fire' two people (either on the basis that they have not contributed much, or alternatively because they are clearly 'carrying' the team too heavily and the other members need to be pushed out of their comfort zone). These two people can become Lord Sugartrader's "eyes and ears" for the rest of the session and provide him with useful insights into how the teams are operating.

Stage 4: Deciding upon the finalists

At the end of this session, Lord Sugartrader will need to decide on the finalists. As far as possible, the teacher should aim to keep one person from each team to go through to the final (although this might not be appropriate and it may be that two people from one team become finalists, and none from another).

To keep the process good-humoured the teacher should start by stressing the positive aspects of the whole team before picking one person out for particular praise and announcing that they are through to the final. It is up to the individual teacher to decide whether it is appropriate to explain why the remaining people are "Fired!".

Make it clear that the 'Grand Final' will take place next lesson.

Stage 5: The final

At the start of the lesson, the finalists should stand up. They are then invited to nominate one person each in the class to form part of their new team. They then choose a second person, and so on, until there are just two people left in the class who have not been selected.

These two people become Lord Sugartrader's assistants: they are given a clipboard each and asked to come to the front of the class to await further instructions.

Part 1: Researching how the slave trade was actually abolished

Each finalist is told what the next last task consists of: namely, they will be directed to two websites which provide a varied list of ways in which the slave trade was actually abolished.

They will have 20 minutes to choose two of these which they think were overall the most effective. Lord Sugartrader's assistants will be taking notes on how effectively each finalist approaches this time-restricted task.

At the end of the allotted time, each finalist should nominate the two methods they have decided to research further and deliver their presentation on. They are then given a further 10 minutes to prepare their brief talk to the class about how and why this particular method was effective.

Part 2: Writing an anti-slavery poem

In the next part of the final, the students are given the first few lines of the anti-slavery poem 'The Anti-Slavery Alphabet'. This is a poem in which each letter of the alphabet refers to a different feature of the slave trade.

Each finalist is then given another batch of the letters (e.g. G-K, L-P, Q-U, V-Z) and then has to produce the next part of the poem in this same format, using their knowledge from previous lessons to help them. These are then read out to the class, and compared to the real poem.

In both stages of the feedback process in this session, it is the teacher's role to ensure that the 'assistants' are encouraged to provide feedback about the quality of teamwork that took place.

It is at the end of this process that Lord Sugartrader announces which student has been "hired" as the successful "Apprentice".

Stage 6: Individual outcomes

It is important at the end of this process that all students produce an individual outcome to consolidate their knowledge. They can do this in one of two ways:

- **Option 1**: Produce a Diamond 9 diagram (page 77) outlining the most important methods by which the slave trade was abolished.
- **Option 2:** Students convert a timeline outlining the process by which the slave trade was abolished into an infographic focusing on one theme, event or individual described within it.

Jigsaw groups

The Jigsaw group technique mixes teams on several occasions during an activity to ensure that students speak to as many people as possible. There are three particularly effective ways of using the method.

Method 1: Each group researches the same narrow question using the same particular case study

The simplest way of organising 'jigsaw' groups is to divide the class into teams, then to give each group the same task, divided between the team members in the same way. For example, each group might be researching the impact of World War Two on the Home Front, and each of the four members in each team looks at this from one angle: economic, political, social and military. Each student researches their area alone for a certain period, then the groups are 'jigsawed' by each person moving to sit with other people in the class who have researched the same theme. After exchanging findings in their 'expert' groups, students return to their original 'home' groups and teach each other about what they have learned.

Method 2: Each group researches the same broad question using different case studies

A slightly more sophisticated approach is to provide each group with the same broad question, and to give each member within it the same angle to look at, but to give each team a different case study to research. For example, the class might be investigating "What are the most common causes of war?". Within each team, different students could be required to research military, social, economic and political causes. However, the crucial difference is that each team will consider a completely different war. In this way, the 'expert group' phase can be much more engaging in terms of spotting comparisons and contrasts and thinking about how best to present these to the 'home' groups later on.

Method 3: Each member of each group researches the same broad question using different case studies

I used this approach to when my students each investigated a different 'historical hero'. For the feedback phase in class, students were organised into groups, and each student in each group was given a number (1-5). The first person in each group was given two minutes to explain to the other members of their group what was so heroic about the individual they researched. When the two minutes are up, the second person takes over and so on until everyone has had a chance to speak.

. The members of each group then have to consider for a few minutes whether they wish to 'stick' with their original character, or 'swap' to one of the others they have heard about. The teacher might even insist that the group has to reach a majority agreement on which character they will all be 'taking forward' into the jigsaw group phase that is due to follow.

The students are then moved into their fresh jigsaw groups in the normal manner, and the process is repeated so that all students can get to hear about a fresh batch of characters. Thereafter they selected a range of characters they have heard about to arrange into a diamond 9 diagram (page 77).

Taking it further
The jigsaw group approach works most simply in the way described above: home group, expert group, then return to home group for feedback.

However, it is possible to arrange things so that a third round of discussion can take place in fresh groups consisting of students who have not yet talked to each other already. To do this, don't just give students in each original group a number to represent their (second) jigsaw group; instead, give them a letter as well to represent a final (third) jigsaw group:

- Group 1: 1a, 2b, 3c, 4d, 5e
- Group 2: 1b, 2c, 3d, 4e, 5a
- Group 3: 1c, 2d, 3e, 4a, 5b (and so on)

In this way, when the jigsaw phase takes place, all the students with the same number sit together as before. But at the end of this phase, another jigsaw phase can take place by asking all the people with the same letter to sit together.

Collaborative essay planning using sticky-notes

In this activity, students summarise their arguments and evidence from research onto sticky notes, put them up on the wall, then categorising and link them meaningfully to work towards an overall synthesis and plan of action.

Example: Why do countries turn towards dictators?

Imagine a group of twelve students investigating the most common causes for the rise of 20th-century dictatorships. Each student researches two dictators from different continents. We therefore end up with plenty of data on 24 dictators from all over the world.

Step 1: Give each student a block of sticky notes. For each of their two dictators, they write three sticky notes explaining the methods they used to get into power. These are then stuck up all over the wall:

Step 2: The class gathers around the board, and are asked to read the ideas that have been shared. Ask them to do this individually and in silence for a few minutes, and to reflect as they do so about which factors are coming up most frequently or which are most closely related.

Step 3: Students are asked to start organising the sticky notes into definable categories. The teachers should monitor this process to ensure that each students has a chance to get involved.

Step 4: Once everyone seems happy with the arrangement, and 'rogue' factors that clearly only applied to individual dictators have been discarded, talked through each category in turn. What do these factors have in common? So what should be the 'title' for each category? Write these titles on differently coloured sticky notes and add them over each category.

Step 5: Discuss how these categories overlap or are connected. 'Psychopathic Tendencies' might be connected to a 'Willingness to use Violence', whilst 'Pragmatic Opportunism' connects to 'Nationalistic Ideology'. These links should explained with annotated arrows.

Step 6: Talk through the clearest 'path' through the completed diagram and discuss how this is effectively a thesis that can be turned into an examination-style essay.

Talkers and listeners

This is an effective way of encouraging close examination of image sources, or close reading of text extracts.

Provide one student (the 'talker') with a source, then another student or small group of students with a series of questions to ask about it (the 'listeners'). The talker is not allowed to show the source to the rest of the group, but must instead simply answer the questions they are asked. When the interrogation is finished, the source should be returned to the teacher. Another member of the group then takes over as the 'talker' by collecting a fresh source from the teacher and the process is repeated.

Example: What was the Medieval conception of Hell?

I use this approach as part of my classroom studies on "Was the Medieval Church loved or feared?". The teacher prints off a pile of Medieval images of hell. The class is divided into groups and each person in each group is given a number. The first person in each group should take one of the images from the teacher, look at it carefully, and take it back to their group.

By looking closely at the image themselves, but without showing it to their teammates, they answer a series of questions about it ("What can you *see* in hell? What can you *hear*? What can you *smell*?"). When the discussion is over (each group can take as much or as little time as they think necessary to take notes), the next 'talker' returns the original picture to the teacher (who scribbles the group name on the back of it to ensure that they are not given it a second time during the exercise), and exchanges it for a fresh picture. The process repeats for as long as the teacher wishes.

After completing the exercise, move to a jigsaw group activity (page 95). Give each student in each group a number (e.g. 1–5). Then instruct all students with the same number to sit at the same table. In this way every group now consists of students who have each used completely different sources of information to their classmates. Give the members of each group a couple of minutes to exchange their findings for each of the key questions and develop their notes with fresh ideas. In this way, everybody in the class will have the opportunity to exchange their ideas with everybody else, either directly in their original groups or by proxy in the jigsaw groups. As a homework exercise, students should use their notes to produce a blood-curdling medieval sermon about the horrors that await sinners in hell!

Discussion group role cards

To ensure that each student is able to contribute effectively and independently during a group task, consider giving each person a different role card:

Creative Risk-taker*   *Everybody should take this role in the first stage of the task to ensure plenty of ideas   You think about the problem critically and rigorously   You think of creative approaches to the task   You share these ideas with enthusiasm
Co-Ordinator (Caring, Principled)   You allocate roles to group members who are unsure what their role should be   You invite each person to contribute their ideas and ensures they are listened to   You pull ideas together at the end in an overall plan everyone is happy with
Elaborator (Inquirer, reflective)   You encourage each speaker to explain their ideas fully   You remind people to provide evidence for their arguments   You help people do these things if they struggle to do so themselves
Researcher (thinker, knowledgeable)   You identify where the group's ideas require more detail and explanation   You are the only person allowed to ask the teacher for information   You conduct the research and provide it to the group
Secretary (open-minded)   You write down the group's findings and decisions without judgement   You ask for clarification and detail from the group if necessary   You make sure the secretary understands your findings
Timekeeper (balanced)   You make sure the group is using the time well   You tell the group when it is time to move on to the next job   You tell the group when it is time to start rounding off
Presenter (communicator)   You ensure you understand what the secretary has written   You present what the group has done to the class and the teacher   You are prepared to answer questions

Template available for download from www.tarrstoolbox.net

Stage 1: individual reflection

Everybody in each team should be a 'creative risk-taker' and have some time to reflect individually on a suggested approach to the task.

Stage 2 : choosing roles

Each member of the group takes at least one of the remaining roles after taking the time to read them (they may choose more than one role). The group will need at least one co-ordinator, who can help the other members decide what roles are important for the success of the task and which are be suited to different members of the team.

Stage 3: group discussion

The co-ordinator(s) chairs the discussion. The elaborator(s) makes sure ideas are being explained fully at each stage. The researcher(s) identify where further research is needed and should conduct this. The timekeeper ensures that the pace of the task is maintained. The secretary keeps a record of the ideas decisions. The presenter(s) are responsible for converting the work of the secretary into a class presentation.

7
TESTS & REVISION

Teaching effectively through the use of classroom games is something I have always been fascinated with. Here are some examples of how fun and entertainment can be brought into the history classroom without sacrificing rigour and focus.

Revision leaderboard

Rather than treat each factual test or quiz as a discrete assignment, foster a sense of competition and tension over the revision period by building up a leaderboard and awarding a prize to the winner.

During revision time I start every lesson with a short factual test, arcade game (page 112) or 'Fling the Teacher' quiz on the topic covered in that lesson.

Prior to the lesson, I warn students what the topic will be so they can revise. At the start of the lesson, I outline the main task for the lesson so they know what to do as soon as they finish the quiz.

I then direct students to a 'Fling the Teacher' quiz on this topic. Students have 10 minutes to complete the quiz.

Any student finishing within that time gets points into their 'leaderboard' (which is an Excel spreadsheet which builds up throughout the revision period) based on the amount of minutes left on the clock. They can then proceed to the main task outlined at the start of the lesson.

It's a great way of encouraging students to do a bit of intensive revision prior to each lesson – especially if prizes are awarded in the final lesson before study leave starts.

"Fling the Teacher" lends itself particularly well to the 'against the clock' format and you can create your own by downloading the free software at www.contentgenerator.net

Keyword challenge

This is a simple game to revise important terms, concepts and people. It is particularly effective just before students have to produce some written work making accurate use of key vocabulary.

Before the lesson, the teacher should put together a list of key terms from the most recent topic of study. When the lesson begins, divide the class into teams of around four or five students.

The first member of the first team sits in the hot seat at the front of the class, with their back to the interactive whiteboard or projection screen.

The teacher inputs the list of key terms into the "Random Word Picker" at www.classtools.net and uses this to display one entry at random on the interactive whiteboard behind the student.

The rest of the team have thirty seconds to get their teammate to guess what word is on the screen behind them by giving a definition.

A correct guess gets points for the team based on how many seconds are left on the clock (e.g. 25 points if they correctly answer after 5 seconds). If 30 seconds elapses without a correct guess, the round is over and the team gets no points.

The teacher should then provide a short outline of the significance of the term, and all students should make a note of it.

The process can the be repeated for the other teams, and the game can then carry on for as many rounds as is the teacher considers appropriate. A prize can be given to the highest-scoring team at the end of the game.

Case study: Was life good or bad in the Middle Ages?

After playing the online interactive Medieval Time Machine adventure at www.activehistory.co.uk and completing the accompanying worksheets, I gave students a list of the main jobs of people that they met in the simulation (scribe, bailiff, apprentice, moneylender…).

Each group had five minutes to work together to revise what each job entailed. They were then told that points would only be won by teams which could not only define the job, but could also explain why it should be regarded as evidence of 'bad' or 'good' conditions. They were then given a further five minutes to consider which jobs fitted which category, and why.

At the end of this period, each student had a list of characters, a brief description of each, and also an inference about what they suggest about the quality of life in the Middle Ages. After we played the game, this then provided useful raw material for either a 'Travel Brochure' for a holiday to the Middle Ages (the task for one half of the class focusing on 'good' elements) or a complaint letter about how the holiday turned into a disaster (the task for the other students focusing on the 'bad' elements).

Random word picker available at www.classtools.net

The pressure begins to tell!

Share possible test questions in advance

Sharing a long list of possible questions with students in advance of a test in exam conditions is a simple way of ensuring that their revision and reflection is focused and effective.

When I tell my students that a forthcoming lesson will be a timed essay or a structured question based on their recent studies, I make a point of sharing with them a list of possible questions that have come up in previous examination papers. I also promise them that the question(s) chosen will be taken directly from that list. Students are then given homework time to reflect on how they might approach each and every question if it turns out to be the one selected. In the following lesson, we spend time discussing approaches to particular questions which they are less confident about. The test then takes place the following lesson.

From my experience, this is more effective than simply announcing that 'next lesson we will be having a test on this topic' and leaving them to revise in an unfocused manner. By giving students a 'long list' of questions they end up preparing much more thoroughly and from many more angles than they otherwise would have done. Moreover, they are able to spot their areas of weakness and have a chance to develop and improve their understanding of these before the test takes place.

Example: World War One structured question (40 minutes)

Instructions: The teacher will choose one (a), one (b) and one (c) question for this test in timed conditions. As homework, all students should therefore consider how they would approach every question in this list.

a. Who was Kaiser Wilhelm II?
a. Who was Tsar Nicholas II?
a. Who was Franz Ferdinand?
a. What were the Balkan Wars?
a. What were the Dreadnoughts?
a. What was the Daily Telegraph Interview?

a. What was the Black Hand Gang?
a. What was the July Crisis?
a. What were the Moroccan Crises?
a. What commitments had European countries made with one another by 1914?
a. What were the Willy-Nicky telegrams?
a. What was the Schlieffen Plan?
a. What was the Russo-Japanese War?

b. Why did the Moroccan crises (1905 / 1911) increase tension between Germany & Britain?
b. Why did an alliance system develop before 1914?
b. Why did an arms race develop between Britain and Germany?
b. Why did the Anglo-French Entente survive?
b. Why were relations between Germany and Russia so tense before World War One?
b. Why was the Triple Alliance formed?
b. Why did Germany issue Austria with a "blank Cheque" in 1914?
b. Why did Russia decide to defend Serbia at all costs in 1914?
b. Why did Britain declare war on Germany in 1914?

c. 'The international crises of 1905, 1908 and 1911 made a general European war certain.' Do you agree with this view? Explain your answer.
c. Why did the 1914 Balkan crisis cause European war, but earlier crises did not?
c. "No country in 1914 actually desired a general European war" – Do you agree?
c. Assess the view that the assassination at Sarajevo made war inevitable.
c. Assess the view that Russia was most to blame World War One.
c. Assess the view that nationalism was the main cause of World War One.
c. Assess the view that Austro-Serbian rivalry was the main cause of World War One.
c. "World War One began because Germany invaded neutral Belgium" – Do you agree?

Spot the mistakes

Summary sheets of key information and facts can be very helpful for students before the examination. To encourage close reading of such resources, deliberately insert mistakes into them and encourage students to find them in a classroom quiz format.

It is always an effective revision technique to provide students with model answers after they have completed an examination-style test (for example, a timed essay). For this reason, I will usually write the essay at the same time as the students, with the only difference being that I give myself 25% less time as a 'handicap' for my experience and speed on my keyboard.

However, from experience I found that one danger in simply providing students with model answers was that they simply got filed away without a great deal of reflection. Therefore, what I now do is deliberately insert factual mistakes into my answers after they are written, and make some stylistic gaffes (e.g. not using paragraphs, quotes or appropriate evidence). I then put students into teams and challenge them to spot the mistakes – which works particularly well if used as part of a 'leaderboard challenge' described earlier in this chapter.

Rules of the game

The first team has to identify and correct an error in the account. If there are a lot of these, insist instead that each team will instead identify and correct two or even three errors.

The team can choose to play for up to 10 points. If they successfully identify and correct the specified amount of errors, they win the points. However, if they fail to do so, or make a mistake, they lose the same amount of points. This rule adds a bit of interest to proceedings!

Everyone in the class corrects their own version of the model answer. The remaining teams then take their turns one after another, and the process can continue for as many rounds as are required.

Taking it further

Get students to produce their own model answers with deliberate mistakes and use these as a 'quiz bank' for future lessons and year groups.

Who, where, what am I?

Students have to identify the most important individuals, events and places related to the topic, then provide five key details about each one. This information is then used as the basis of an intensive group quiz.

Stage 1: preparatory revision and research

In advance of the lesson, students prepare quiz cards designed to challenge the other people in the class to guess a key character from the topic about to be revised. The quiz cards require the student to provide five statements about the character, each one of which is progressively more obvious who it relates to.

Stage 2: conducting the quiz

After collecting the quiz cards, the teacher arranges the class into teams and shuffles the pack. The "50 point" statement will be read out from the first card to the first team (obviously, the teacher will need to choose a card that wasn't designed by a person within that team). If they wish to 'pass', they get further (easier) clues but the points available steadily decline (40 points for a correct guess after the second question, 30 points after the third, and so on).

An incorrect guess at any point means they automatically get zero points for that round and the card is placed back into the pack – so it usually a good idea for each team to nominate a 'captain' who is the only person allowed to give the quizmaster the final answer after conferring.

The game is played over several rounds; the winning team is the one with the most points.

Taking it further

The rules of the game are flexible. Most simply, each team could take it in turns to guess a different character from the five statements they are provided. However, another approach is to adopt a 'first on the buzzers' approach using some quiz buzzers. I also record the scores from these quizzes in a revision leaderboard which builds up over several weeks of revision to build up a bit more tension, as outlined at the start of the chapter.

Answer buzzers add an extra layer of tension to a classroom quiz and can be purchased on Amazon.

Arcade game generator

The arcade game generator at www.classtools.net allows you to submit one set of questions and answers and then converts these into a range of interactive revision games. Each of these can be shared as web links or embedded in a website, blog or wiki.

To create a game, simply input a series of questions and answers into the interface (these can easily be copied and pasted directly from an existing worksheet).

At the time of writing, the games generated currently include:

- Manic Miner
- Wordshoot
- Cannonball
- Matching Pairs
- Flashcards
- Asteroids (2-player option available)
- Pong! (2-player option available)

Several of the games include a leaderboard so that at the end of the allocated time the teacher can see the highest scores attained by each student.

Taking it further

- Create a leaderboard during revision time (page 104).
- Get students to create their own revision games on different subjects ahead of the revision period. Use this databank of quizzes as starter/plenary exercises during revision time, and compile a revision leaderboard to build up a sense of competition.
- There are other game generators available at www.classtools.net, including the PacMan Generator, Only Connect, and the HTML Crossword Generator.

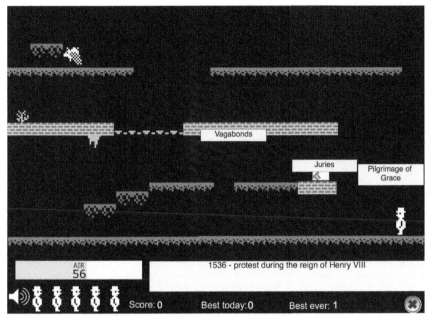

Manic Miner: Jump onto the correct answers to move up a level

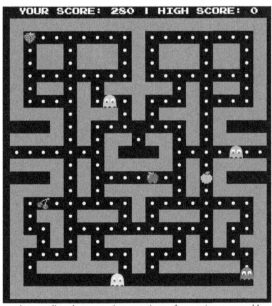

Pacman: win extra lives by answering questions after getting captured by a ghost

8

CLASSROOM DISPLAY

Classroom displays, even when changed regularly, often have little educational value since students regard them as the equivalent of wallpaper or visual static. What follows in this chapter are a variety of suggestions about how to make your history classroom displays both visually appealing and educationally valuable.

Who tall are you?

The 'Who tall are you?' poster is designed to be printed off on A3 paper, laminated and then placed at the appropriate height in the classroom.

Students (and teachers!) are invited to stand against it and write their names at the appropriate height to find out which historical celebrities share the same height.

The 'who tall are you?' resource can be downloaded at www.tarrstoolbox.net

Lesson / activity idea

Each student in the class should measure themselves against the 'Who tall are you?' chart.

Each student then has to choose one of the names corresponding to their height to research in more detail.

The teacher will then conduct a 'balloon debate' between the different characters over several rounds to determine the most important character chosen.

Taking it further

The "Who tall are you?" chart can be taken down at the end of each academic year and replaced with a fresh version. As students make their way through the school it will be interesting to chart their growth over the course of their time at school over several years.

"Inspirational quote" posters

Get students to locate a thought-provoking quote about a topic, theme, or by a person related to the current topic, then turn it into a classroom poster. Display one poster per week on your classroom door to provoke some reflection and discussion.

Case study

As a development of my study unit on "Who is your history hero?", I challenged my students to locate a thought-provoking quote by or about their chosen character, or alternatively a quote about one of the 'heroic' qualities which they identified (determined, creative, principled and so on). Students can easily locate inspirational quotes from websites like www.brainyquote.com. Next, students used the free service at www.canva.com to turn their quote into a poster. I then rotated the best posters as a "thought for the week" display on my classroom door.

Taking it further

Students could be encouraged to provide an observation on the quote by leaving a block of post-it notes nearby. These can then be turned into follow-up quotes from the students themselves so that the "quote of the week" turns into an on-going conversation. I've started doing this with the display outside my own classroom after one of our students wrote a post-it note in reply to a Martin Luther King quote, and I then turned this into the following week's poster.

As an extension activity, students could research the author of the quote and provide a brief biographical summary as part of the poster and a web link or QR code with further information.

Classroom windows as word walls

With classroom space limited, consider building up a 'Word Wall' on available windows or glass doors.

Window crayons can be purchased cheaply at online stores such as Amazon. Whenever a new or interesting word crops up in discussion or through reading, add it to the wall.

Taking it further

- Consider having separate word walls for different year groups.
- The word wall can be used for regular lesson starters.
- With younger classes, invite a different student each lesson to ask for a definition of one of the words added by the older classes.
- With older classes, challenge students to construct a sentence using different words from the wall in relation to the topic currently being studied.

"Currently being studied" posters

Maintain a 'currently being studied...' area outside the classroom, with separate A3 laminated posters outlining topics being studied by each year group.

Each poster consists simply of the key enquiry question and a relevant image. When one topic finishes, simply take down the old poster, keep it aside ready to use again next year, and replace it with the new one.

This display technique not only gives younger students an interesting insight into the sorts of things that they will study later on in their exam years, but also enables colleagues in other departments to spot potential overlaps with their own study topics.

This in turn can inspire fruitful conversations leading to cross-curricular projects between various subjects.

Taking it further

Ask students themselves to design the poster as an extension task. What image will they choose? What key question will they identify?

Students could design the posters using the 'Breaking News Generator' at www.classtools.net.

Sample 'currently being studied' posters

Share video projects with QR codes

Many students enjoy the challenge of producing a video project to consolidate their learning. QR codes are a simple way of sharing these with the wider school community.

The main drawback with video projects, in comparison to posters or written work, is that they do not easily lend themselves to display.

To get around this problem, simply save the video on the web or on a page of your school's virtual learning environment. Next, use Google's URL shortening service (www.goo.gl) to get a short web address of this location. Even better, when you click the 'details' option you are given a QR code that you can copy directly into a document.

Print this information onto a piece of paper, place it on display and then students can scan the code to watch the film (QR scanning apps can easily be found for free in the ITunes store or similar). These can then be placed on your classroom door.

Students scan the QR code with their mobile phones to watch the video

Taking it further

Another great feature of the Google's URL shortener is that if you are logged in to your Google account when you use it, you can get a quick summary of how many times it has been watched, along with other information.

"In the news...!" posters

In order to reinforce the relevance of History, and to encourage students to engage with current affairs, have a regular "In the news..." notice pinned up on the door outside your classroom.

I set aside a regular slot each week where I check my favourite blogs and newspaper websites for articles relating to my subject (I collate these using the excellent online service www.feedly.com), then print out the most interesting and stick them up on the classroom door along with a suitable title or question for consideration.

To save time, you can also set up Google Alerts (www.google.com/alerts) so that you can receive immediate email updates regarding any mention in the news of key topics and individuals relevant for your subject..

Students will often read these during their break periods of when they are waiting to come into class, and this will generate discussion at the start of lessons.

Taking it further

The same approach can be adopted using TV listings to highlight particularly useful television programmes that will soon be broadcast.

I have created an automated service which identifies the most recent history-related news, podcasts and blog posts which can be accessed at www.activehistory.co.uk/newhistory.

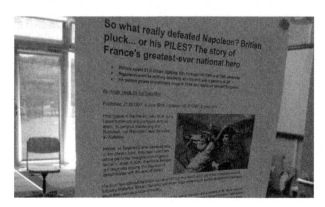

"Open me" display pieces

When producing a display poster summing up several ideas, students should identify a 'cover image' for each main part of the piece. This should be 'lifted up' to expose the written detail.

These sorts of display pieces are a good way of associating an essential image with each piece of relevant information, and of encouraging students to engage with the display rather than ignoring it as if it were simply wallpaper.

A sample 'open me' display piece on the culture of the Weimar Republic

Taking it further

An even simpler method is to take a piece of A4, fold it in half to create a greeting card, and place the image on the front with the written information inside. I have done this when students researched the origins of superstitions: a bold illustration on the front (e.g. of a four leafed clover) and an explanation on the front. A class collection of these forms a good display.

Acronyms and icons

For revision purposes, creating memory words, with each letter representing the first letter of another key word, helps students construct an effective way of recalling a larger amount of information.

At the start of a topic too, it can also be used as a technique for encouraging students to read the text more closely and actively reflect on fresh knowledge.

Step 1: Summary words
After identifying key factors, events, causes or effects, challenge students firstly to provide a one-word summary for each one.
For example, here is a summary of 6 problems facing the Peacemakers in 1918. Students need to add a heading in each box to summarise its message (e.g. "Rash bargains", "Deadly Disease" and so on).

Problems facing the peacemakers in 1919	
??	??
The war ended very suddenly. This meant that there was no agreement between the allies about how Europe should be reorganised. It also meant that ordinary Germans were left completely "shellshocked" by their defeat – why had they surrendered when their army was further into France than it ever had been?	The War had created political chaos across Europe. The monarchies of Russia and Germany had been overthrown. The Austrian and Ottoman Empires had disintegrated as national minorities started forming their own new countries (e.g. Czechs, Slovaks, Serbs, Bosnians, Poles).
??	??
The Allies had made rash bargains with countries such as Italy and Japan, promising territory after the war in return for their support. Would they have to stick with this?	Voters put pressure on the democratically elected leaders – the English and French public wanted to "Hang the Kaiser" and the Americans wanted a return to "Isolationism".

??	??
The war had completely changed the balance of world power. The war cost Europe $260 billion dollars, much of which had been loaned by the USA, which emerged as the world's first and only superpower.	An influenza pandemic was raging across Europe. Ultimately, this killed more people (c. 30 million) than the war itself! Half of the US soldiers who failed to return died of the 'flu, not from enemy action!

Step 2: Acronym for revision

An acronym is a word made up of letters, each of which symbolises another word. For example, the ADVENT verbs in French are those which take "Etre" in the past tense (aller, devenir, venir, entrer, naitre, tomber). Students have to now produce their own acronym of 6 letters to summarise the six titles they came up with earlier. They may have to change some of these so that they have a selection of letters from which you can make a word (i.e. a combination of consonants and vowels).

Example: The Treaty of Versailles

For the Treaty of Versailles, I get students to remember the acronym "TRAWL' (**T** = Territory | **R** = Reparations | **A** = Armaments | **W** = War Guilt | **L** = League of Nations)

Then within this, I encourage students to remember the "SCRAP" over Territory (**S** = Saar | **C** = Colonies | **R** = Rhineland | **A** = Alsace-Lorraine | **P** = Polish Corridor).

Step 3: Adding an icon

Students can add an appropriate icon in each box to summarise its message. I encourage students to think in terms of road signs and map symbols. For example, how can you summarise each of these factors as an image?

Problems facing Hitler after he became Chancellor in 1933		
Parliament	Party	Presidency
Hitler was only chancellor of a coalition government – of its 11 members, only 3 were Nazis!	The SA was becoming difficult to control. Its leader, Ernst Rohm, was starting to challenge Hitler's leadership	President Hindenburg had ultimate control. He deeply distrusted Hitler.

9

ESSAY SKILLS

The knack of writing a good essay in a subject like history is a skill which is a challenge to acquire for many students, but immensely rewarding and useful. The ability to carry a reader along with a well-crafted argument is no easy feat, since it involves carefully synthesising the creative arts of the storyteller with the scientific rigour of the evidence-driven empiricist. This chapter provides several techniques for helping young historians develop these vital skills.

Visual essay-writing in groups

This multimedia approach allows students to conduct an investigation by organising various sources into categories and then linking them together to produce the basis of an essay plan.

To develop analytical and essay-writing skills in a collaborative and engaging manner, start by gathering a series of photographs relating to the topic in question:

- A pile of cartoons and photographs (maybe about 20 of these)
- Podcasts
- Video clips
- Textbooks
- Articles

Next, divide the class into groups. Within each group, three students should be responsible for organising the cartoons into meaningful categories to answer the key question for the lesson (in the photograph shown overleaf, cartoons are being organised into meaningful categories to help understand "Why was the Marshall Plan so controversial?").

Whilst the 'cartoonists' are busy discussing how to arrange the images meaningfully, another student should be listening to the podcasts, another watching the video, another reading the article, and another reading a textbook (it is a good idea to let students choose the task they are most comfortable with, as far as possible). As they spot any evidence that helps answer the key question, they should write it on a sticky-note (this helps them to keep their points short and focused).

When the cartoonists have finished organising their images into categories that make sense to them, the next step is to give each category a heading, and to link the categories together in a meaningful manner by spotting causal links and natural overlaps. At this stage, I get different cartoonists to swap places with the someone in another team, the members of which then explain their diagram to their 'visitor'. Each person then returns back to their original team and makes suggested amendments based on any bright ideas gleaned from the other team or teams.

At this stage, the readers/viewers/listeners will start to be joining the cartoonists, bringing their sticky notes with them. Their job, working with the team, is to discuss the answer that appears to be emerging, and to determine where to place their sticky-notes to best effect to help provide the essential detail to give substantiation to the ideas identified in the cartoons.

Thereafter, each group can compare and contrast the answers that they have formulated, before each individual student provides a formal written response to the key question using their completed diagrams to help them.

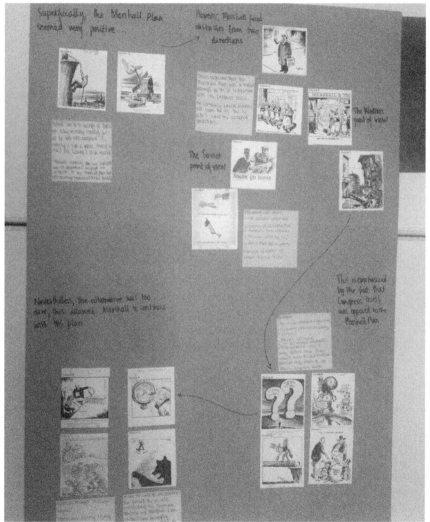

A sample outcome investigating the motives behind the Marshall Plan.

Taking it further

The visual essay writing approach overlaps effectively with the hexagon approach (page 23) and the sticky-note approach (page 97).

Write a script, not an essay

Giving students an essay to write as the main outcome of a unit of study can be repetitive and tiresome. To give students a fresh enthusiasm for essay writing, present the topic instead as a documentary-making project.

This approach has additional benefits in the sense that it stresses the art, not just the science, of essay writing. By recording themselves as part of the process of making the actual film, it also gets students to reflect carefully on how their own voices come across and the importance of speaking clearly, steadily and lucidly when presenting to an audience.

Case study: making a film on the causes of the American Civil War

Phase 1: Students gather information about the topic
In my case, my study of the causes of the American Civil War begins with a teacher lecture, then an illustrated timeline task whereby students start to build up a folder of high-resolution images based on the most interesting events and developments. They also research events in more detail by watching clips from the famous Ken Burns documentary.

Phase 2: Students consider how script writers construct a narrative
I do this firstly by watching Ken Burns being interviewed on "The Art of Story" (available at www.vimeo.com) which is a brilliant synopsis of how the historical writing process is a balance of science (empiricism, research) and art (imagination, emotion). We then watch the opening minute of several documentaries to see how they use silence, subtle music, carefully chosen images and a narrative 'hook' to engage the viewer from the outset (in particular, I use the opening segment of the first episode of "The World at War" which is fantastic in this respect).

Phase 3: Students select and connect the main factors
In this phase students are effectively writing their essay, but they are seeing this merely as one part of a creative process and are much more engaged. They start by choosing the five most interesting events in their timeline and

explain how each one increased the tensions which erupted into war. Next, they have to connect these factors in five key sentences using "connectives" ("As a result...Nevertheless...This meant that...This highlighted...This accelerated...This was the result of...Because of this..." and so on). Following this, they have to develop each sentence into a full paragraph with substantiating explanation and detail. Finally, they have to design their own narrative 'hook' to serve as an introduction, and decide how to round the story off.

Phase 4: Students record the script create the film

In this phase, we start with a lively and humorous discussion about what usually marks out school film projects as being amateurish. Students usually identify such things as a monotonous, rushed, mumbling narration, irrelevant and low-resolution images and intrusive background music. These are clearly therefore the things to avoid! Students record their narratives into Audacity, import these into IMovie or similar, and then overlay the images they gathered in Phase 1 to produce their movie.

		Marks
Structure	Narrative structure [1-2] or analytical structure [3-4]?	1-4
	Engaging introduction and a thought-provoking conclusion	1-2
Research	Detail from classroom notes [1-2] or also from personal research [3-4]?	1-4
Visuals	Related to the narrative	1-2
	Good range, good resolution	1
	Subtle motion / transition effects	1
Narration	Clearly spoken and recorded at a sensible pace, with varying intonation to maintain viewer interest and appropriate use of silence	1-4
Music	Sensibly chosen backing track used to add atmosphere, at a suitably low volume	1-2
Total		20

Sample mark scheme for a documentary script project

Banned word list

As a history teacher there are certain tired words and phrases which make me wince when I see them being used by examination students. I therefore use my classroom window word wall (page 118) to list words and phrases which are not only useful, but also those which I do not want to see being used.

Structured questions

My key banned phrase for topic sentences in essays and structured questions is "On the one hand...on the other hand" (the ultimate 'fence-sitter' response). In this way, during test conditions and in homework, students have a ready list of useful 'balancing phrases' which express a meaningful position ('Although, in some minor respects,....Nevertheless, more fundamentally...') without creating written pieces which appear non-committal.

Source work questions

Another window in my classroom has a similar list of words to help students evaluate source material. Here, the banned phrase is 'This is a primary source so it is reliable because....this is a secondary source so it is reliable because...' - the classic stock response in source work questions for students that can't be bothered to reflect properly on the particular sources they are presented with.

In this case, I provide students with other words. During revision time I ask them to rank these from words which suggest 'most reliable' down to 'least reliable'. Once again, this helps students broaden their vocabulary and provide a more nuanced response to examination questions. For example, how would you rank these words in that manner?

Partial	Contradictory	Impartial
Biased	Ill-informed	Objective
Partisan	Well-informed	Subjective
Prejudiced	Propagandistic	Secondary
Bigoted	Censored	Primary
Vitriolic	Edited	

Rubric grids

To help students improve their essays skills, I consistently use the same rubric sheet to provide them with feedback on different aspects of their performance and progress.

Students are graded against the following separate criteria, giving an overall total out of 20 marks:

Name of Student: Title of Essay:						Comments
	L1 - 1 Mark	L2 - 2 Marks	L3 - 3 Marks	L4 - 4 Marks	Bonus Mark	
Introduction / Conclusion	Introduction 'sets the scene' and outlines what factors will be considered. Conclusion summarises the main points made in the essay.	Introduction 'sets the scene' and summarises what the essay will seek to prove. Conclusion summarises the main points made in the essay and establishes clear lessons for what this topic provides for today.				
Structure	Narrative Although not incoherent, the essay is a narrative account of events with very little analysis.	Narrative with bolt-on analysis There is some limited analysis, but the response is primarily narrative/descriptive in nature rather than analytical.	Opening paragraph sentences are arguments, but do not link together consistently. The response makes appropriate links and/or comparisons although these are not always convincing.	Opening paragraph sentences are arguments, and consistently link together consistently to provide a balanced 'path' of argument. Arguments are consistently clear, coherent and effective in terms of links and/or comparisons.		
Breadth	Key factors overlooked There is limited understanding of the demands of the question. Key aspects of the topic will be completely overlooked	Lack of balance between paragraphs There is sound understanding of the demands of the question. The most important aspects of the topic will be covered, but not in a suitably balanced manner	Lack of balance within paragraphs There is good understanding of the demands of the question. The most important aspects of the topic will be covered in a suitably balanced manner. However, there is little awareness of different perspectives and concepts within each paragraph.	Excellent range and balance Responses are clearly focused, showing a high degree of awareness of the demands and implications of the question. There is rigorous evaluation of different perspectives and concepts, and this evaluation is integrated effectively into a sophisticated answer.		
Depth	Limited use of classroom materials The essay relies on partial use of classroom notes. The relevance of this knowledge is not always established.	Good use of materials Appropriate evidence is drawn effectively from classroom notes and / or wider reading. This is used to substantiate the arguments being presented.	Excellent use of evidence, used illustratively Plenty of evidence is also used from wider reading (e.g. quotes, historiography, statistics), but is taken at face value AND/OR a bibliography is not included.	Excellent use of evidence, used critically (its reliability is regularly questioned) The examples used are appropriate and relevant, and are used effectively to support the analysis/evaluation.	Any candidate in Level 3 or 4 gains an additional bonus mark if they include a bibliography AND footnotes in their essay.	

Full-scale template can be downloaded at www.tarrstoolbox.net

For each of these, I provide different level descriptors for 1 mark up to the maximum available for that particular essay feature. Then, it's simply a question of shading off the correct cell in the grid and providing an explanation on the right-hand side.

The benefits of this approach are that I mark the essay much more methodically, but also much more quickly. Rather than make one overall evaluation right at the end of the essay, I instead make separate, shorter but more focused comments about half a dozen features of the piece. This provides the students with feedback which is directly comparable to their previous essay rubric so they can spot exactly where they have improved, and where they need to focus next.

Miscellaneous essay approaches

It is not enough to simply take in an essay, mark it and provide feedback, and then hurry on to the next lesson or activity. Much better is to take in a first draft of the essay, involve the students in some reflection and redrafting, and then take it in for final marking so that the advice is immediately being put into effect rather than going stale whilst the class awaits the next essay assignment several weeks later.

Listed here are a few activities that can be used to help students improve their essay-writing skills after their initial draft of work has been completed.

1. Analysis skills for students

The Skeleton
Students should produce an essay plan which contains merely the first topic sentence of each paragraph. This should then be passed to a partner, whose job is to suggest what evidence could be used to substantiate the point made by each topic sentence.

Objection!
The teacher takes a completed essay and reads out just the opening topic sentence of each paragraph to the class. If at any point anyone in the class thinks that an opening sentence is a narrative statement of fact rather than an analytical argument they should say "objection" and explain why. The sentence should then be developed appropriately before moving on to the next.

Flowchart
Students are organised into pairs. One student reads out the opening topic sentence of each paragraph and the partner has to summarise the overall argument in the form of a flowchart to share with the class. A poorly constructed essay will consist of simple narrative statements and this will be more difficult to achieve, whereas a well constructed essay will consist of

analytical statements, linked together in a logical way.

2. Narrative skills: "Mr. Interpretation"

One student reads out a sentence of factual detail from an essay and nominates somebody else in the class to provide an analytical point that it illustrates, for example:

- Person 1 presents a fact – "Tsarina Alexandra was German by birth"
- Person 2 the interpretation – "Provides explanation for opposition to Tsar during World War One"

If the nominated person explains the significance of the fact successfully, it is their turn to choose a factual detail of their own and nominate somebody else. If they fail to explain the significance of the fact, they are knocked out of the game. The winner is the last person standing.

3. Source evaluation skills: "Mr. Sceptical"

This is the same as "Mr. Interpretation" except a third person in each round has to show an awareness of the limitations of the evidence:

- Person 1 presents a fact – "Tsar Nicholas was 'not fit to run a village post office' (Trotsky)"
- Person 2 the interpretation – "Provides explanation for opposition to Tsar during WW1"
- Person 3 the limitations – "But Trotsky was a hostile witness", "But the Russians were deeply loyal to the principle of Tsarism".

4. Challenging the question: "Mr. Angry"

Students are provided with a list of sample questions from past exam papers. For each one, they have to explain:

- What loaded assumptions are within it.
- Why these are quite obviously completely and utterly wrong.

5. Structural skills: where are the paragraphs?

The teacher should take an article available in a digital format (e.g. from the History Today archives), paste it into a Word document, and then remove all of the paragraph marks and (as a final act of stylistic sadism) make it 'fully justified'. Students should then be presented with this essay from hell, and challenged to deduce by reading it carefully where they think that each of the original paragraphs began. This can then lead into a discussion about how a writer determines when to start a new paragraph – for example, when they are about to make a brand new point in relation to the question, or take the previous point in a fresh direction.

6. Avoiding stock responses: "Rewrite a model essay"

Students should be given a model essay or an article on a key topic. They should then examine past exam papers to determine what other questions have been set on this theme. In what ways, and to what extent, would the given essay need to be re-written and re-structured to answer these questions?

7. Focusing on the command terms: "Guess the title of the essay"

Another technique is for students to copy and paste the entire article or essay into a word cloud website such as www.wordle.net or www.tagxedo.com. If a writer has clearly focused on the command terms then these will appear at a higher frequency in the word count and therefore will be displayed more prominently in the word cloud.

8. Only use quotes you disagree with

Using quotes in essays is too often a technique used by students to avoid thinking for themselves. Worst of all is the paragraph which is effectively a potted summary of another writer's point of view. To avoid this, students should be asked to remove any quotes which they actually agree with. Instead, they should use quotes as a means of setting up a debate and demonstrating clear evidence of independent thinking ("Although AJP Taylor argued that…this does not bear close scrutiny because…").

10
OTHER IDEAS

This chapter provides a miscellaneous range of thoughts about such things as homework strategies, rewards and sanctions, and cross-curricular projects between history and other subjects.

Choose your own homework

Giving students the flexibility to choose the content and / or the outcome of their homework assignments increases engagement and promotes independent learning.

When the teacher gives the class an open-ended opportunity to reflect on what they need and want to learn about, and then to choose the most effective way to demonstrate their learning, students are able to take more ownership of their studies and teachers are able to cover more material in a more diverse manner. Another appealing aspect of this approach is its ease of implementation: it does not have to be adopted wholesale for all year groups and all homework assignments, but can rather be adopted to different degrees and at the most appropriate times. This is an approach which has been popularised particularly by Ross M. McGill (@teachertoolkit – see his blogpost at http://goo.gl/QMNbvj) and Mark Creasy (@EP3577). The hashtag #TakeAwayHmk is used on Twitter to share ways in which the approach has been used.

Example 1: "choose your own content"

The simplest way to get started with a "choose your own homework" approach is to allows students the freedom to choose their topic of study, but for the teacher to specify the outcome. In this way there is flexibility in terms of content, but the teacher will be able to measure some distinct skills through the work that is produced. I use this approach with my older students at the end of the first half term, when I set them a holiday homework designed to get them thinking about the possible focus of their extended essay assignment. I give students a list of recommended podcasts (e.g. "Great Lives", "In our Time", "Witness" and "The Moral Maze", all of which are freely available from the BBC). Their job is to listen to at least one hour's worth of podcast material, and then use this to deliver a classroom presentation on one or more key questions raised by what they have learned. Example presentations that resulted ranged from "What are the main causes of the Arab-Israeli conflict?" to "How has game theory informed international decision making since World War Two?".

Example 2: "choose your own outcome"

My IGCSE History students reached the end of a heavily detailed and methodical study of Hitler's foreign policy in the 1930s with a desperate desire for some creative, independent work. I therefore gave them a homework which consisted of producing a resource designed to demonstrate their understanding of the key questions relating to Hitler's foreign policy in such a way that they would find it a useful revision aid. I made it plain that the only rule was that the outcome clearly demonstrated thought and effort and would prove useful as preparation for the final examination. I then gave the class some time in groups to list some possible outcomes, then we shared these as a class.

The range of proposals was immense, including such things as a Google Earth Tour of the key locations of conferences and clashes relating to Hitler's foreign policy; a 'Diary of a Wimpy Fuhrer' outlining the main steps towards World War Two in the form of an illustrated children's book; a "TripAdvisor™" review of each place coveted by Hitler from his perspective, complete with rating to indicate its importance; a photo-album scrapbook of a German soldier from the 1930s charting the progress of German foreign policy; changing the lyrics of a song to cover the topic essentials in a way that would be memorable, and much else besides.

Open homework outcomes on Hitler's foreign policy

Example 3: "choose the content and the outcome"

The most open-ended method of all, of course, is to give students the flexibility to choose both the topic and the outcome rather than merely one or the other. I tried out this approach recently with a class that was studying the growth of the British Empire. I provided students with a summary grid, with the main periods of growth forming the columns and the main countries and products involved forming the rows. Their job was to produce a homework based on one cell of the table (a particular event), one row (which focused on one of the key countries involved) or one column (which focused on one particular period). In this way they had a great deal of flexibility to choose a task corresponding to their interests and abilities. For example, the students who tended to focus on a single cell (event) in the table either did so because they wanted to keep the task more manageable, whereas others who did so opted for it because it addressed a key issue that stimulated their interest: a Dutch student investigate in more depth the occasion when the Netherlands sailed its ships up the Thames in a daring raid in 1667, for example.

	When?	Where did they settle?	What products did they gain?	Who settled in this area?	Why did this happen?	Who were they rivals with?
West	1610s	**North America** They settled in Virginia (named for Elizabeth I) and married native American women like Pocahontas	**Tobacco** Tobacco and coffee was imported into Britain from North America.	**Pilgrims** The Pilgrim Fathers sailed from England on the Mayflower	**Protestants** They wanted to escape from persecution in England	**France** British settlements in North America threatened French settlements in Canada like Quebec
	1650s	**West Indies** Pirates like Captain Morgan used their riches to establish sugar plantations in Jamaica	**Sugar** Sugar was imported into Britain from Jamaica. Most was re-exported to Europe, making Britain wealthy	**Pirates** Captain Morgan stole gold from Spanish galleons coming from the "New World"	**Catholics** They wanted a Protestant Empire in the "New World" to rival that of Catholic Spain	**Spain** British pirates attacked Spanish ships in America. The British seized Jamaica from Spain in 1665
East	1660s	**Indonesia** Trade bases were established in places like Bantam in Java	**Spices** The "Spice Islands" of Indonesia sold pepper, nutmeg, cloves and tea to the British	**Merchants** The East India Company was established to establish trade links with Asian countries	**Economics** Gold, tobacco and sugar generated wealth for the British, who wanted to spend it on Asian spices and clothing	**Holland** The "Spice Wars" with Holland saw Dutch ships sail up the River Thames towards London in 1667
	1750s	**India** The British established trading bases which became the cities Bombay, Madras and Calcutta	**Clothing** India provided cotton and silk which was immensely popular in Britain	**Politicians** Robert Clive exploited and then defeated the ruler of India at the Battle of Plassey	**Politics** The Mughal rulers of India sided with the French during the Seven Years' War - so the British attacked them	**France** Britain defeated France in the Seven Years' War. Britain now "ruled the waves" and controlled trade out of India

Open homework starting point on the British Empire

Bounce the detention

This is a simple strategy that I have used for many years when students need to work silently for a period of time. All that's needed is a prop which can be passed from one student to another (I use the large foam die that always lies around my classroom when I need to randomly choose a group to answer a question).

The rules are straightforward. The class needs to work in absolute silence. Anyone talking or otherwise disrupting anyone else in the class during the allocated time will receive the foam die and get a five-minute detention where they will have to practice sitting in silence.

However, if anybody else subsequently breaks the same rules, then the original detainee is completely off the hook and the detention (and the foam die) passes instead to the new offender, who now faces a detention that has increased to six minutes.

From my experience, the original detention sometimes 'snowballs' upwards for a little while (five minutes for Rohan...six minutes now for Noah but Rohan you're off the hook...seven minutes now for Rory, but Noah you're free...), but then hush will quickly descend as the cost of breaking the rules becomes the loss of an increasingly large slice of their free time.

Like any disciplinary strategy it is of course crucial that the rules are made absolutely clear from the outset, and applied firmly but fairly. I always deliver it with good humour, and stress that it is in order to help the students work more productively for a clearly defined period of time. As a result I often get classes asking to 'play a game of bounce the detention!' when they spot themselves that productive discussion around the tables has degenerated into irrelevant chatter.

Create bookmarks as rewards

Design a range of subject-themed bookmarks, print them off, laminate them and cut them out as prizes for good work.

The great thing about these bookmarks is that you can use a permanent marker or a pen for writing on CDs to put a brief congratulatory message on the back to pass to the student. Over time, students could be encouraged to 'collect the set' or even design some themselves as a homework project.

I have created a wide range of these bookmarks which you can download freely from www.activehistory.co.uk.

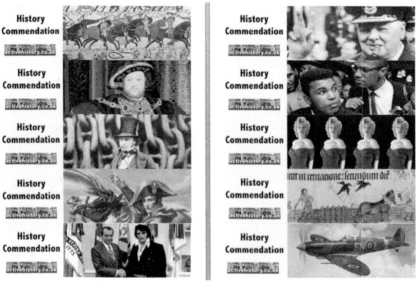

Bookmarks downloadable from www.tarrstoolbox.net

Hands up if you DON'T know

One of the most common, and maybe one of the very worst, teaching techniques is to say to students "Hands up if you can answer this question".

This is because the same (confident and able) students end up hogging the lesson and the rest of the class simply falls below the radar: either happily (because they'd rather have an easy life) or unhappily (because they might like to get involved but lack the confidence of the others). Put simply, the act of raising a hand requires a degree of self-confidence that many able but shy students – especially younger ones – lack. And if the teacher chooses to ignore the students straining with their hand in the air to encourage a less confident student to offer an answer, a sense of injustice and resentment can result.

With this in mind, consider taking a new approach. Instead of asking students to raise their hand when they DID have something to contribute, they have to raise their hand to express that they DID NOT have anything to say or to ask. This requires you to re-frame my questions: instead of "Who can tell me...?", ask instead "Who is NOT able to tell me...?". I then had to choose the students who had not raised their hands.

This might flummox the class to start with, but in a good way. Those students who wish to stay 'under the radar' now have to counter-intuitively raise their hands; those students who usually hog the discussion have to keep their hands down; but so too do the more shy students who feel they know the answer. These students can now be asked to contribute points without the more pushy students feeling they had been unfairly ignored.

One proviso applies with this method: if you frame a question in such a way that highlights ignorance, then of course nobody will be willing to raise their hands ("Read through the following passage. If there are any words you don't understand, raise your hand and I'll explain them"). So once again, reverse the question. Place the students into small teams, then encouraged them to read closely by asking the following question instead: "Raise your hand in a few minutes if you are confident you can define ALL of the words in this account. Points will be *given* to any students who can identify a word which NOBODY in the class can correctly define". All of a sudden, students will be searching for words that they do not understand with enthusiasm instead of trying to hide their lack of knowledge and understanding.

Cross-curricular speed-dating

One of the biggest challenges in a school curriculum is to break down the barriers that students and teachers set up between their various subjects. Too often, students treat each subject in isolation instead of realizing how skills acquired in one area are transferable to another.

An quick way to spot links between curriculum areas is a cross-curricular speed dating event between staff lasting for as little as one hour. The ideas generated can be fed into curriculum review discussions or used for curriculum-crossover projects.

Start by arranging the room with two chairs on either side of each desk. Divide the staff into groups of six teachers, with no single group containing two members from the same department:

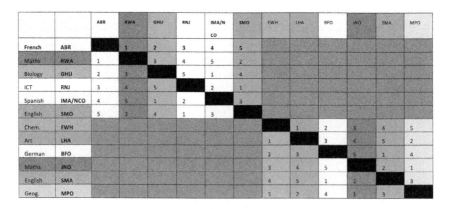

		ABR	RWA	GHU	RNJ	IMA/NCO	SMO	EWH	LHA	BFO	JNO	SMA	MPO
French	ABR		1	2	3	4	5						
Maths	RWA	1		3	4	5	2						
Biology	GHU	2	3		5	1	4						
ICT	RNJ	3	4	5		2	1						
Spanish	IMA/NCO	4	5	1	2		3						
English	SMO	5	2	4	1	3							
Chem.	EWH								1	2	3	4	5
Art	LHA							1		3	4	5	2
German	BFO							2	3		5	1	4
Maths	JNO							3	4	5		2	1
English	SMA							4	5	1	2		3
Geog.	MPO							5	2	4	1	3	

Each group can then be arranged into three pairs around three desks, and then simply rotate clockwise one place in a musical chairs format over five rounds lasting 10 minutes each. Each of these 10-minute sessions should be structured as follows:

- 5 minutes: Each pair of teachers aims to identify at least one key topic, and one key skill, that overlap between their subjects.
- 3 minutes: Each pair of teachers writes down their findings (even better, record them in a Google form).

- 2 minutes: Each teacher moves clockwise around their table of six people to face their new partner.

The process can then be repeated over five rounds. The results generated in the Google spreadsheet provides a rich mine of inspiration to be shared with all staff and for curriculum development, two examples of which are provided below from my own school.

Outcome 1: What was the most important development of the Renaissance?

Students are organised into teams which carousel through a series of one-hour specialist lessons (e.g. Geography, Science, Art, Design and Technology, ICT, Maths, Music). In each lesson, the teacher will address two questions:

a. What changed during the Renaissance in this subject?

b. Why did these changes take place?

The following morning, the students have two hours to produce presentations to answer the "Big Question":

c. What was the most important development of the Renaissance?

Finally, the groups deliver their presentations to the school principal, who judges the overall winner. In addition, each team "peer assesses" itself to determine who contributed most to the success of the team.

Outcome 2: Was World War Two a period of progress?

In the first week back after the summer holidays, students starting the IB are placed into teams and take part in a themed event involving six subject groups. Teachers involved in the event provide a one-hour lesson investigating the positive and negative legacies of World War Two in relation to their particular subject specialism.

Co-ordinators involved in the event then help each team of students tie these various lessons together in an overall thesis which forms the basis of a group presentation, which is judged by senior teachers. This is then followed by each student writing an essay which marked according to a strict rubric, the results of which are recorded in the student reporting system as a baseline assessment.

Local history scavenger hunts

Scavenger hunts are superb not just for developing awareness of local history, but also for team building. In this sense they are a great way to start the new school year, when many new students might be joining the school.

Stage 1: Complete the first mission

Students are taken to the centre of the local town and are divided into small teams. Each team is initially given a mission sheet consisting of a series of questions and challenges that can be answered by visiting different places hinted at in various clues. For example, the first challenge for our students in Toulouse is "Go to the gardens nearby which are named after the French Resistance leader during World War Two who later became President".

Toulouse Treasure Hunt		
Tick the final column for any tasks you achieve!		
As your first task for 5 points, take a photo of your team in front of the Mairie.	📷	
🏃 Proceed to the gardens behind the Mairie. This square is named after the man who led the Resistance Movement in World War Two and who then became President afterwards.		
Take a photo of yourself in front of the monument to this man.	📷	
Locate the modern sculpture of the mother and child in the same square. What is the name of the sculptor?		
Locate the monument to a Toulouse mayor assassinated in 1914 for 'non-patriotism' when he resisted the drift to war with Germany. What was his name?		
🏃 Head straight through the middle of the gardens until you reach the main road named after a province of France regained from Germany		

Opening tasks in the scavenger hunt used as part of the induction process for IB students at the International School of Toulouse

Once they arrive at this spot, they are asked to complete two tasks. Firstly, they are asked to answer a factual question by looking around the place in question ('Find a monument in the gardens dedicated to a local mayor assassinated for refusing to support France's war against Germany in 1914, and write down his name here'). Secondly, they are asked to take a group photo at a particular spot nearby ('Find the sculpture of Resistance leader after whom these gardens are named, and take a group photo alongside it'). For each task completed, the team will gain a point.

Stage 2: Complete the remaining missions

From this point, the 'proceed to a place' format can be repeated indefinitely: I used Google Maps to identify 10 key places around the city within walking distance, and then created a series of questions which guides them through clues from one place to another ("Proceed through the gardens till you reach a road named after the province regained by France at the end of World War One. Head West down this until you reach a square named after England's patron saint" – and so on). It is a good idea to ensure that each question, as far as possible, works in isolation rather than requires successful location of the previous spot: in this way, if students are unable to work out where they need to go they can cut their losses and move on to the next challenge instead.

Stage 3: Beat the clock!

One crucial ingredient of the treasure hunt is to provide a strict time limit. Teams have to hand their completed sheets back to their quizmaster at the designated location before a specified time (so that we can all get on the coach on time, as much as anything else!). Failure to do so incurs a heavy penalty or even disqualification. In this way, an element of urgency is built into the event. There is always one teacher based at a central location in case students need to locate them urgently, and we also provide each group with the school mobile phone number.

Taking it further

- It is not helpful to have all the teams following each other around in one large clump. Therefore, design the route in a broadly circular format consisting of several mystery locations (e.g. "Location A"

145

through to "Location F"). Then, give each team a slip of paper which gives the actual name of a different particular place in the mission, and the question that it corresponds to in their activity pack. Each team then proceeds to its nominated locations and then works through the questions from that point forwards (with the final question in the mission pack directing them back to "Location A"). In this way, all the students rotate through the locations independently and the chance of them following each other around is minimised. It also ensures that all of the key locations will be visited, which is important for the class debrief when students return.

- Include useful bits of trivia about the places in question so that when groups arrive there they can learn additional interesting things about them. In particular, names of streets, buildings and squares are a rich and generally untapped historical source.

- Set some 'selfie challenges': provide students with a photograph of a local landmark – complete with some interesting information about it - then ask them to take a group photograph at this spot to earn bonus points. One particularly fun task is to get students to find a statue in the area commemorating a famous figure, then use a 'face swapping' app on their phones to take a bizarre picture alongside it.

Acknowledgements

During my almost twenty years in the classroom I have been inspired by countless other history teachers. It is impossible to name them all here, but I would like to give a special mention to a handful of exceptionally generous history-teaching colleagues who regularly share ideas on Twitter.

Name	Twitter handle
Scott Allsop	@MrAllsopHistory
Carmel Bones	@bones_carmel
Richard Byrne	@rmbyrne
Clare Bracher	@cjabracher
Leanne Davison	@HistTeach1989
Ian Dawson	@BearWithOneEar
Alex Fairlamb	@lamb_heart_tea
Larry Ferlazzo	@Larryferlazzo
Andrew Field	@andyfield
Alex Ford	@apf102
Anne Gripton	@gripgirl
Terry Haydn	@terryhaydn
Johnny Hemphill	@worcesterjonny
Kate Jones	@87History
Richard Kennett	@kenradical
Lesley Munro	@lesleymunro4
Lesley Ann McDermott	@LA_McDermott
Sean McDermott	@SeanwelshBacc
John Mitchell	@jivespin
Patrick O'Shaughnessy	@HistoryChappy
Ed Podesta	@ed_podesta
Michael Riley	@Michaelshp
Tom Rogers	@RogersHistory
Carol Stobbs	@littlestobbsy
Dave Stacey	@davestacey
Sally Stevens	@sallyluane
Sally Thorne	@MrsThorne
Greg Thornton	@MrThorntonTeach
Ilja van Weringh	@vanweringh
Ben Walsh	@History_Ben
Glenn Wiebe	@glennw98
Victoria Hewett	@MrsHumanities

For a more comprehensive list of history teachers on Twitter please visit my web page www.activehistory.co.uk/historyteacherlist. You can also search Twitter using the hashtags #historyteacher (UK), #histedchat (Australia) and #sschat (USA).

ABOUT THE AUTHOR

Russel Tarr has a degree in Modern World History from Lady Margaret Hall, Oxford University and a PGCE from Birmingham University. He is currently Head of History at the International School of Toulouse, France.

He is author of the award-winning www.activehistory.co.uk, which provides innovative resources and online simulations for the history classroom, www.classtools.net, which freely provides online game generators and learning templates, and www.tarrstoolbox.net, which shares practical classroom strategies for teachers.

Russel delivers training courses to history teachers in the UK and Europe, writes regularly for the national and international press on historical and educational issues and is a prominent figure in the educational community on Twitter (where he tweets as @russeltarr / @activehistory / @classtools).

Printed in Great Britain
by Amazon